"Winnie-the-Pooh never explains what he means by 'the noise-you-make-before-beginning-a-piece-of-poetry'. But in this glorious gallimaufry Stewart Henderson allows us an insight into 'the noise-the-poet-makes-before-writing-one'. *A Poet's Notebook* gives us a glimpse inside the mind and the muse of the poet, the rhapsodic rattlebag from which each individual poem coalesces out of chaos."
PAUL VALLELY, former executive editor of *The Independent on Sunday* and author of bestselling biography, *Pope Francis: Untying The Knots*

PRAISE FOR STEWART HENDERSON'S POETRY:

"Essential reading"
The Sunday Times

"He understands the packed power of words; the importance of their use and measure"
Gillian Reynolds, radio critic, *The Sunday Times*

"Has the capacity to engage naturally and touch deeply"
Christine Morgan, Head of Radio, BBC Religion and Ethics

"What Michael Morpurgo has done for children's fiction, Henderson has done for poetry"
Melanie Carroll, *The Church Times*

"Good-humoured, thoughtful poems"
Roger McGough, CBE

T0341458

A POET'S
NOTEBOOK

WITH NEW POEMS...
...OBVIOUSLY

STEWART HENDERSON

LION

Published by
Lion Hudson Limited
Wilkinson House, Jordan Hill Business Park,
Banbury Road, Oxford OX2 8DR, England
www.lionhudson.com

ISBN 978 0 74598 032 4
e-ISBN 978 0 74598 033 1

First edition 2018

Acknowledgments

Back cover image of Stewart Henderson © John
de Garis
Cover image © Dirk Wustenhagen/Trevillion
Images
p. 5 Extract from "Harrow-on-the-Hill" in
Collected Poems by John Betjeman, published by
John Murray. Copyright © 1958 John Betjeman.
Used by permission of Hodder and Stoughton.
p. 15 Extract from "May my heart always
be open to little" in Selected Poems by E. E.
Cummings, published by W. W. Norton &
Company. Copyright © 1994 W. W. Norton &
Company. Used by permission of the publisher.
p. 17 Extract from "Prayer" in Mean Time by
Carol Ann Duffy, published by Anvil Press.
Copyright © 1993 Carol Ann Duffy. Used
by permission of Rogers, Coleridge & White
Literary Agency.
pp. 33-34 Extracts from "Authentic Creativity
vs. Karaoke Culture" by Malcolm McLaren.
Copyright © Malcolm McLaren, Handheld
Learning, 2009, TED.com. Used by permission
of TED.com.
p. 36 World except US: Extract from "And Death
Shall Have No Dominion" in Twenty-Five Poems
by Dylan Thomas, published by J. M. Dent
and Sons Ltd. Copyright © 1936 The Trustees
for the Copyrights of Dylan Thomas. Used
by permission of David Higham Associates.
US: Extract from "And Death Shall Have No

Dominion" by Dylan Thomas, from The Poems
of Dylan Thomas. Copyright ©1943 by New
Directions Publishing Corp. Reprinted by
permission of New Directions Publishing Corp.
p. 41 Quote from the episode "Survival – At
What Cost?" from the programme After Dark,
broadcast 19 January 1991, produced by Open
Media. Copyright © 1991 Open Media. Used by
permission of Open Media.
pp. 60, 90 Extracts from "Snow" and
"Autobiography" in Collected Poems by Louis
MacNeice, published by Faber & Faber.
Copyright © 2016 Louis MacNeice. Used by
permission of David Higham Associates.
p. 73 World except US: Extract from "The
Hollow Men" in Collected Poems: 1909–1962
by T. S. Eliot, published by Faber & Faber.
Copyright © 1925 T. S. Eliot. Used by
permission of Faber & Faber. US: Extract "The
Hollow Men" from Collected Poems 1909 – 1962
by T. S. Eliot. Copyright © 1936 by Houghton
Mifflin Harcourt Publishing Company.
Copyright © renewed 1964 by Thomas Stearns
Eliot. Reprinted by permission of Houghton
Mifflin Harcourt Publishing Company. All
rights reserved.
p. 127 Quote from Of Time and the City, written
and directed by Terence Davies, produced by
Hurricane Films. Copyright © 2008 Hurricane
Films. Used by permission of Hurricane Films.
p. 149 Extracts from "Scotland" in Inside Out:
Selected Poetry and Translations by Alastair Reid,
published by Polygon, an imprint of Birlinn
Limited. Copyright © 2008 Alastair Reid. Used
by permission of Birlinn Limited.
p. 150 Extract from "The Academy" in
Weathering: Poems and Translations by
Alastair Reid. Copyright © 1978 by Alastair
Reid. Published by Canongate Publishing Ltd,
Edinburgh, Scotland, 1978. Used by permission
of The Colchie Agency.
p. 185 World except US: Extract from "The Milk
Factory" in Opened Ground by Seamus Heaney,
published by Faber & Faber. Copyright © 1998
Faber & Faber. Used by permission of Faber &
Faber. US: Extract from "The Milk Factory' in
Opened Ground by Seamus Heaney, published
by Farrar, Straus & Giroux. Copyright © 1998
Farrar, Straus & Giroux. Used by permission of
Farrar, Straus & Giroux.

A catalogue record for this book is available
from the British Library

This book can only be for my darling Carol
(please see chapters 19 and 21 especially).

Without her, many of the poems would not have seen light,
nor would this book have been shaped.

Enough said… but not nearly enough said about her…

CONTENTS

FOREWORD

Here's the good news: the words of mine you are reading right now will be the least interesting in this entire book. And I'm including the ISBN number. The sentences won't always have meaning, and the grammar needs paying attention to. Everything else in this book is much better, so you have all that to look forward to.

The blame for the comparatively poor quality of this foreword lies partly with me for not being a better writer but largely with Stewart Henderson. Stewart is such a magnificent writer, observer of humanity, poet and Judy Garland impersonator that my best efforts – and believe me this is my best effort – are but a sideshow; an appetizer; an...er...introduction.

I'm doing this because Stewart asked me to. I imagine he hopes that my fame and acknowledged celebrity status will sprinkle some stardust and bring perhaps a few extra sales. Let's face it, books with poems in them need all the help they can get. Books with writing about the poems as well as the actual poems are little short of box office poison, so I'm happy to do what I can with these words. I wondered why he didn't bestow the honour on other famous people he knows, but of course they're all dead.

How do I know Stewart Henderson?

At a roast of the American comedian Don Rickles, his pal, American comedian Bob Newhart, said this: "Don Rickles is my best friend. Which just gives you some idea of the difficulty I have in making friends."

I won't insult Stewart by claiming to be his best friend, and he isn't mine. That honour belongs to Alexa. Then Siri. *Then* Stewart.

I first met Stewart when he appeared on a radio programme I was presenting in Glasgow. In my memory he looked exactly the same then as he does now. I think he also has the same coat. Either he hasn't aged or he's always looked like a man in his sixties.

His recollections of our first and subsequent on-air encounters are more vivid than mine, and he writes about them in this book, generously saving his mentions of me until he's almost out of material at the end.

I liked him from the start because I could ask him anything and he would always come back with something better. He performed brilliantly, and off-air possessed a quiet dignity and calm that made him stand out amid all the hubbub. This book is all about what Stewart understands of the world through his willingness to stop and listen and hear and think.

We worked together several more times over the years, sometimes with Stewart toiling as my producer. He was the best producer: answering my questions before I could ask them and displaying a quite shocking degree of diligence. Nothing was left unconsidered.

His first class professional care and diligence is nothing compared to who he is as a person. Speaking as a man who can be difficult to get to know, Stewart's kindnesses, apparently intuitive understanding of how human beings work, and unwavering support continue to sustain me. We get together for dinner a few times a year and these evenings are always a highlight.

If this premature eulogy I am writing gives the impression Stewart has saint-like qualities, I should also say he makes me laugh uproariously, has Liverpudlian "shoulder", and it's fair to say you would want him at your side in a street fight.

An email from Stewart is a double-edged virtual sword. He writes so well that even his sign-offs should be compiled and written in a book. My replies pale. His sharp mind and even sharper pen cannot help but illuminate everything they touch. So you are in for a treat with this book. After all, this is a man who knew Malcolm Muggeridge and almost met Sir John Betjeman.

This is a man who admits in this very book, "I've taken extensive notes about enjambments, dactyls and elisions", so you know you're in good hands.

In reading this book, I realized I didn't know about ninety-eight per cent of what Stewart has done so far in his life. His words moved me to tears of all kinds (except for "Fears") and I have no hesitation, as a bona fide celebrity, in recommending it wholeheartedly to you.

I wish he had written this intro for me, but there we are.

Eddie Mair, presenter, *PM* and *iPM*, BBC Radio 4

Listen to your life. See it for the fathomless mystery that it is. In the boredom and the pain of it no less than in the excitement and gladness… because in the last analysis all moments are key moments, and life itself is grace.

Frederick Buechner, ***Now and Then***

ACKNOWLEDGMENTS

I would like to express my great thanks to Ali Hull for instigating this book, steering it through to editorial acceptance, and for believing in me. I would like to extend that gratitude to Jessica Tinker, Joy Tibbs, and Kirsten Etheridge in particular for inheriting the project and so ably and carefully ensuring that this book did, in fact, "become".

"Eyes Down" was commissioned by, and first broadcast on, *Good Morning Sunday*, BBC Radio 2, 2015.

"Anfield, Winter – 1960" was written for, and performed at, The Creative Unconscious – Psychoanalytic Poetry Festival, Anna Freud National Centre, 2015.

"Under the Clock" was recorded for the album *Because We Can,* by Martyn Joseph and Stewart Henderson, Pipe Records, 2005.

"… Be the…" was adapted for the song "The Luminous Years", subsequently recorded by Gareth Davies-Jones for the album *The Beauty & The Trouble*, Heading West Music, 2017.

"Everything in Heaven Comes Apart" first appeared in the collection *Limited Edition*, published by Plover Books, 1997, and was subsequently recorded for the album *Because We Can*.

"Thunder and Rainbows" first appeared in the collection *Still, facing Autumn*, published by Plover Books, 2001, and was subsequently recorded for the album *Because We Can*.

ABOUT THIS BOOK

What to write about this book? I could write a whole book on the subject "about this book", making it a two-volume speciality act. But, as I can hear my editor weeping at the thought (and she's over fifty miles away – panic, like sound, travels), I will limit myself to a manbag of illustrative quotes from others and let your interest read on… or not. It's your life, free to spend as you wish. To quote my beloved wife, Carol, this book is more "a kaleidoscope of jottings": part journal, part rummage sale of the mind that ended up in the twenty-one poems that conclude each respective chapter.

But please don't put this book down with the lame generalization "I don't understand poetry". That, to me, is the same as saying, "I don't understand speech or conversation… and whatever." Allow me to patronize you: poetry is a different way of talking, without the "ums", "ers", and "you knows".

At its best, poetry is precision speech that speaks of more. I don't understand brain surgery but I marvel at those who dare to open the human skull to correct impairments. Such precision-surgeons have spent their lives perfecting their skills; that is what these supreme technicians have chosen to do with their lives. In a more minor way, in the operating theatre of the psyche, the surgery of poetry can, if not heal, then certainly alleviate, at times, a malfunction in the head or heart, or both. Vocational poets have studied their manuals and applied their knowledge – and, like Dr Jekyll and Mr Hyde, drunk their own potions (sometimes to their own detriment).

Samuel Beckett saw language as a veil: in other words, the Irish playwright employed other words to underline his meaning. (Interestingly he wrote *Waiting for Godot* in French because he found more clarity in the Gallic language.) He considered that which is written, spoken, or heard is a gauze. A not-the-full-story. A work-in-progress, a partial expression, possibly containing temporary clarification. Well, that's what I think he meant. I could well be wrong. It wouldn't be the first time I've barked up the erroneous Scots pine.

I have spent all my adolescent and adult life attempting to coax out from behind the veil – through, primarily, poetry, as well as song lyrics, prose, and radio scripts – approximations of sense and insight. My exercises in accessible, precision speech. My own wee parables, as opposed to mission statements – from which I usually recoil. Whereas the parable continually reveals, the mission statement too often enshrouds its adherents in static legalism, the very opposite of its initial intention. At its best, poetry's precision speech… speaks of more. The veil momentarily lifted, the gauze transfused with light.

The Scottish poet Kathleen Jamie likened the writing of her anthology *Jizzen* (old Scottish word for "in labour") to completing an examination and then walking into the welcoming sunshine. The writing of poetry is a playground and a seminar, running concurrently. Participation in both is required but not one at the expense of the other. In the living is the noticing and imbibing, which in turn becomes the poetry; "the common language heightened", to quote Gerard Manley Hopkins. In effect, poetry is conversing from a loftier perch while waiting at the bus stop.

Poetry, the reading and writing of it, has sustained this particular ravenous heart and mind. It has been a helpmeet – tranquillity in the turbulence of life's "brick through the window" calamities. I have tried to pass that sustenance on through my books, performances, and broadcasts. Poetry has served as counsel and an equilibrium, guiding me away from those threatening times of total emotional implosion. Poetry is for the "I alone" and the "we together". It has also enabled me to, echoing the first text-speak poet, e. e. cummings, "do nothing usefully".

This book is about memory, forgotten recall, and how the past inhabits us more as we geographically move away from it. This book is especially about paradox and faith; the interrogating of and deciding to follow, sometimes reluctantly, the latter. The book is also about immersing oneself in the trust of paradox, in its depths of buoyancy.

The sacramental poet Anne Ridler, who worked for T. S. Eliot at Faber & Faber in the years before the Second World War, wrote that "Poetry… is a discipline… that helps one to face hard truths". Bardic sister Kathleen Raine regarded poetry as being about "the service of life" in order to magnify the "more intense sense of the beautiful". To that I would venture my contribution to this poetic triptych; appropriate verse can soothe us in the aftermath of our terrible, traumatic violations, in partnership with germane therapy.

Priest-poet R. S. Thomas also reminds me that rabbiting on too much about what a poem means, or could mean, does not necessarily ensure its effectiveness. So I've tried to avoid that.

The preceding essays to each of the twenty-one poems are, I hope, informative and reflective accounts of the disparate, and in some cases direct, influences that brought the poem from behind the veil. Important contributing aspects such as the context of location and individuals known, or never personally encountered, should win best supporting actor for this production.

The poems are about the usual suspects – life, death, and the spaces and arcades in between, with their accompanying experiences of bewilderment and serenities. In the poems you should find jokes, jaunts, and the contemplation of distress and resignation at the perpetual folly, shadiness, and impurities of power: power being that aphrodisiac with its coronations of buffoons, tyrants, the studious, the well-meaning, and the bereft.

Ultimately, this book is about how poetry – the word incensed by the Word – has been, and will continue to be, for me, a way of breathing and being in the attempted service of readers and listeners.

EYES DOWN

From where does inspiration come? In a huge variety of ways – both sublime and prosaic.

For our present Poet Laureate, Carol Ann Duffy, it happens through the late night and early morning shipping forecast on BBC Radio 4 when "the radio's prayer… utters itself". This incantation of sea areas surrounding these islands, rising and rolling like the ocean, an almost hypnotic rhythm of place names stimulating our imagination *to see further*, a removal from the here and now to a *far away beyond*… "Fisher, German Bight, Humber… Malin, Hebrides, Bailey," intimating adventure and danger… "There are warnings of gales…" This nautical invocation, taking the listener out into the unknown where there may even be a limitless horizon…

Meanwhile, back on dry land…Vauxhall… Clapham Junction… Earlsfield… Wimbledon… Raynes Park…

I, too, can summon a geographical cadence: in my case, a lilt of place names as city becomes suburb, eventually transforming into a grand arrival at the former palace of Henry VIII. A litany of railway stations from London's Waterloo to Hampton Court, also taking in spectacularly unexciting New Malden, and Jerry and Margo Leadbetter's domestic nirvana of Surbiton – not forgetting Thames Ditton and the Anglo-Saxon settlement of Berrylands, famed for its present-day water treatment plant. Book early to avoid disappointment.

This is a journey I have taken many times over the past thirty years, there, back, and on my way to creative ventures involving radio, film, television, and poetry performances.

A former Poet Laureate, Sir John Betjeman, was also stimulated by the mobile muse of the train. His 1973 BBC documentary, *Metro-Land* (directed by BAFTA-winner Edward Mirzoeff), was a verse–prose hymn to the rail and tube network that brought the outlying expanse of Middlesex, Buckinghamshire, and Hertfordshire into London's reach in the early years of the twentieth century. Betjeman's graceful and germane eye documented the daily lot of the pre- and post-war commuter heading home from Baker Street to privet-trimmed Pinner and elsewhere – and, if there was time, the treat of a short repast or beverage in the station buffet. Betjeman's equivalent "New Malden" was Neasden, "home of the gnome and the average citizen".

Metro-Land has stayed with me down the years, mainly because of Betjeman's use of poetry as "everyman reportage". The brisk line, the lingering observation, the small meditation on the individual's place in the scheme of things as city clerks and secretaries are confronted by the many moods of God: "When melancholy Autumn comes to Wembley", the opening line of "Harrow-on-the-Hill". Accessible metaphysics while approaching Chorleywood, with the perennial, nagging anxiety that permeated Betjeman's verse – that perhaps God keeps a detached and non-interventionist distance from us all. So let's all ponder that universal isolation at the Communion rail and get on with things as best we can. Mustn't grumble; we'll just write private poems in those moments of quiet despair.

And although Betjeman's poetry might read now as a chronicle of a particular type of an almost-disappeared Englishness, a preparatory and public-school, sepia Albion, the glee, gloom, and tribulations in his work are general and timeless.

Some years following the initial broadcast of *Metro-Land* I wrote an article examining the "elevated ordinary" in Betjeman's poetry, highlighting the mournful ecstasy and dashed depths he experienced through unrequited, and passing, love – a common theme in his poetry.

Having completed my epic, I sent the published outcome to Sir John via his publisher, "Jock" Murray. Being the eminent and astute editor that he was, Murray gave me a few notes concerning the highs and lows of my earnest piece, especially the lows. A few weeks later, however, a typed note arrived signed by Sir John in a vulnerable shaky hand, thanking me for my "thoughtful" writing with additional well-mannered sincerities, and plaudits too. A generous and treasured acknowledgment from an ailing man (as he was by then) to an unsolicited correspondent. Having kindly suggested we meet, sadly he died some weeks later, in the spring of 1984, before such a longed-for encounter could take place.

Depending on the etiquette of one's fellow travellers, a train journey can invoke contentment, contemplation, or lament, sometimes all at once, bringing about the transformation of carriage into cloister in which to ponder and pursue the varying tempos of poetry.

A queue of poets has allowed their thoughts from a train, with its speeding and stationary views from the window, to speak through them and to us. Most famously, perhaps: Edward Thomas at "Adlestrop", where it is forever "late June". Equally recalled is Philip Larkin in "The Whitsun Weddings" mulling over the Lincolnshire landscape's merging with the firmament. And further down the twilight tracks, the harrowing metaphor in "The Send-Off" by Wilfred Owen, of boy-men conscripts singing "their way to the siding-shed".

Whatever the terminus, the train also doubles up as the means to an anticipated embrace or a forlorn goodbye wave. "On the Departure Platform", following a kiss at the barrier, Thomas Hardy's love is left, getting "smaller and smaller... until to my view she was but a spot".

The train and station has also had its ticket punched as a leading character in popular fiction and film; to name a few, *The*

Thirty-Nine Steps, Brief Encounter, Murder on the Orient Express, and Harry Potter at King's Cross bound for Hogwarts from Platform 9¾.

Ever since George Stephenson's *Rocket* locomotive, complete with multi-tube boiler, reached a bone-shuddering 24 mph at the Rainhill Trials in 1829, the train has become a means to individual and collective altered states; not just a jolly day-excursion to Leamington Spa, but also a journey into our known, and, at times, unknown consciousness where "a trance of being" is interrupted by the bagatelle banging of the refreshment trolley coming up the aisle.

My train-inspired poem that follows at the culmination of this chapter, "Eyes Down", had one important and practical contributing factor: its genesis was a commission from Janet McLarty, producer of *Good Morning Sunday* on BBC Radio 2. Janet and I have worked together very creatively and happily on several programmes, including an hour-long Radio 2 documentary on suffering, *Where Was God?*

Janet's experience and skill as a producer meant that when a couple of years ago she asked me to "please write something – anything you like" for *Good Morning Sunday*, my immediate response was "great" while she added the all-important producer-proviso "so long as it's, ideally, no more than one minute twenty seconds". Radio, rightly, because it is a finely tuned and edited medium, does not do "reams". I had been on the programme before so I knew the form.

That conversation between Janet and me had taken place in the BBC studios at Media City in Salford. I was there for one of my regular gigs – choosing, writing, and presenting duties on *Pick of the Week* for Radio 4. Having been privileged to complete that enjoyable task, I toddled down to the Religion and Ethics department a couple of floors below to catch up with colleagues with whom I've worked in the past. And that is how, sometimes, commissions come about. As the much-missed late Justin

Phillips, former Deputy Editor of *The World Tonight* on Radio 4, said to me once, "often it's just a case of 'happening to be there' at the right moment".

On the final leg of my trek home from Salford, I was turning over Janet's request as I boarded at Waterloo, bound for Hampton Court. As the rush-hour train trundled out of the station, ancient and modern landmarks gleamed in the sublime summer evening. The London Eye – first cousin to the Riesenrad in Vienna's Wurstelprater amusement park in the 1949 film *The Third Man* – was a giant's sparkling orb; Big Ben – Pugin's last Gothic Revival hurrah before physical and mental breakdown consumed him in 1852 – a tower of intricate completeness. The evening sun blessed and encouraged both these architectural wonders with radiance, a benediction on the best and most brilliant of human design.

But it was the skyscape that started to dictate the poem: a staggering gift of early-evening shade and splash, cumulus constructions of shift and subtlety, a reckless palette of praise and elation.

Astonishingly, however, virtually to a person, inside the carriage, heads were dipped. The cords of headphones hanging, wisps of techno-dreadlocks bowing down – a hot and exhausted, disconnected group. Outside we were being given glory without realizing it, and, in a manner, ignoring and squandering it.

For me the poignancy of this separation from the bounty over us was further exacerbated in the immediate aftermath of the recent terrorist mass-shooting of thirty-eight people and wounding of many others at Port El Kantaoui, a few miles north of Sousse in Tunisia. Hence the juxtaposition of the images of cute cats and carnage in the poem. By journey's end the poem was virtually complete.

"Eyes Down" can be interpreted on several levels, one of those being that we are not as a broadly speaking, self-immersed society in the best shape to combat external tumult. In avoiding rigorous inner scrutiny and engagement with the random mayhem of our times, retreat, or just shouting, becomes the wholly "reasonable" course… leading much to our further spiritual diminishment.

The poem seeks to serve through, I hope, psalm-like qualities; or, dare I suggest, it is a modern-day psalm with poetic elements – my technical stimulus being the original Old Testament Psalms, which were and are compact expressions and examples of the Hebrew poetic canon, and which provided insight by means of sacred word and sound acrobatics for the contemporary listeners of *their* day.

EYES DOWN

We are the eyes-down generation
tapping on apps and icons,
scrolling for signs and wonders,
cradling our tablets of capricious stone,
our soothing and desolate slabs
with their images of singing kittens
and shrouds on beaches;
an indiscriminate kinetic canvas,
a potpourri gallery of
the deplorable and the frivolous.

We are the eyes down generation,
and… Bingo!… If we follow this link
we will have won something…
Really…?… How generous… how crooked…
Beware – pickpockets operate
in this touch-screen area.

We are the eyes-down generation.
But if viewed from above,
how do we appear?
A cloistered congregation on buses?
Hunched-over mystics on trains
wired-up for solitary, sing songs
and numbing news?

We are the eyes-down generation
pining for glory
and mourning our looted innocence.
Meanwhile we do not hear the untethered clouds
as they chorus to us… pleading…
 "Look up… look up and consider…
all this has been entrusted to you…
so that you do not look down."

2

"TRAGEDY, ECSTASY, DOOM"

The poem at the end of this chapter is a response to various viewings, over the years, of the American Abstract Expressionists in galleries in London, New York, and Boston, and in particular, Mark Rothko. Although identified with that pre- and post-Second World War artistic movement, Russian–Jewish émigré Rothko ignored such "group photos", and splashed away with fervour, seeing choice of colour as the key element in his work – the metaphorical club membership card being an irrelevance, and a restriction.

However, the poem possibly started – miles to go, and far away – decades earlier, in my home territory.

In the Walker Art Gallery in Liverpool hangs *The Funeral of Shelley* by Louis Edouard Fournier, completed by 1889 when the French artist was in his early thirties.

The oil-on-canvas scene depicts the "Godless poet" Percy Bysshe Shelley, neatly stacked on a burning funeral pyre at the ocean's edge.

Shelley had drowned in the Gulf of La Spezia off the north-west coast of Italy in July 1822. He was aboard his schooner *Don Juan* when the vessel encountered rough seas. The poet and two others, friend Edward Williams and deckhand Charles Vivian, went down with the vessel, their bodies washing ashore several days later.

To borrow a latter-day saying, Shelley, infamously, "didn't do God". The Romantic poet's truculent stand against the prevailing and respectable theological tenets of his time were bugled in his essay-cum-tract "The Necessity of Atheism" while a student at University College, Oxford. Such a scandalous, negative affirmation repudiating conservative absolutes in matters divine led to him being sent down (expelled) in 1811. Shelley had previously made known his distaste for "the structure" when at public school he refused to submit to the "odious and degrading custom" of fagging.

Up until then it had all been going so well in a superficial kind of way: son of a landowning Whig knight, Eton educated – a dilatory pupil but with a developing poetic consciousness. His "outsider" reputation helped to broaden his literary fellowship, which, in time, brought him into the licentious domain of fellow "up and out" visionary Lord Byron.

Shelley went on to pen, or should that be quill, some epic verse, including "Ode To The West Wind", "Ozymandias" (the deft sonnet on the transience of power), and his beyond-himself consideration of the firmament, "To The Moon", in which he tenderly asks our neighbouring satellite, "Art thou pale for weariness/Of climbing heaven and gazing on the earth/Wandering companionless/Among the stars that have a different birth…?" Lines worthy of due and lasting meditation: a four-line seminar on how to transform everyday words into illuminating profundity.

Following the reports of Shelley's death, a Tory newspaper of the day, *The Courier,* in high, and somewhat uncharitable, dudgeon taunted the expired radical, "Shelley, the writer of some infidel poetry, has been drowned, *now* he knows whether there is a God or not." Shelley, obviously, was not in a position to return a libertarian right of reply. Shame really, as it remains absorbing conjecture as to what irreligionists past and present make of their afterlife state, or non-state, should they demand the wish to carry over and hold to the logic of their earthly views, despite the possibility of the challenging contrary.

Yet Shelley's rebellious stance subsequently ensured his legacy as a frock-coated poster boy for the still, mainly, received view of poets – awkward, mardy, defiant, pacifist, thin-as-wishbones, promiscuous, human counterpoints, impractical, and in Shelley's case not someone with whom to embark on a merry sail around the bay.

Of late, I was reunited with Fournier's portrayal of Shelley's demise following my wife Carol's loving encouragement that we should have a jaunt to Liverpool after several years' absence from visits to the homeland, and head to "The Walker", in particular.

On viewing the cremation scene again after forty years, I was struck by how the moody theatre of the spectacle had remained, albeit dimly, in the far canvas of my memory. However, subsequent reading in the long interim period about the lives and works, and respective diaries and letters of, Shelley, Byron, and another of their circle, Leigh Hunt, meant that I was, in a manner, viewing the painting for the first time. While Fournier's piece is an artistic opera, a sombre, haunting evocation of "the dying of the light", the painting is, seemingly, not factually true. It may well be artistic licence beyond the call of improvisational duty.

Without wishing to completely erode the spirit of the painting with invasive literalism, in Edward John Trelawney's *Recollections of the Last Days of Shelley and Byron,* Trelawney, a sort of derring-do maritime adventurer (some would say chancer), befriended the dynamic duo, and so was in a position to identify Shelley's body, and was further cast in the role of ad hoc stage manager of the pagan ceremony. Although Trelawney only knew Shelley for a brief period, he later traded on his "I was there" cachet, accepting the task of selectively editing the poet's letters prior to posthumous publication.

Fournier's painting shows Byron, under a mourning, winter-like sky, watching his friend become ash, with poet Leigh Hunt and Trelawney a few paces away. If we are to believe the account recorded by the accomplished anecdotist and polished myth-peddler Trelawney, on the day of the cremation Leigh Hunt remained in his carriage and Byron, perhaps overcome in the weird way grief affects, absented himself from the depressing proceedings, going off to grieve by way of a swim. The August weather on the day also was far from grim; it was reported by Trelawney as the opposite, hot and generally sultry. Trelawney's "recollections" were published in 1858, thirty-six years after Shelley's death, and later revised in 1878, under the title *Records of Shelley, Byron and the Author,* three years before Trelawney's own death. If Fournier had read Trelawney's dispatch, then he chose to ignore the witness statement.

There are further historical inaccuracies in the painting, such as Shelley's second wife, Mary, represented kneeling in the background: an unlikely instance given her perilous health at the time, as she was recovering from a miscarriage. Also, it was not the received custom then for wives to attend their husband's funeral.

Allowing for Trelawney's first-person testimony, and some scholars' accusations of his "embroidery in hindsight", paintings like poems *can still* arrest us in that first moment we encounter their power, irrespective of their factual authenticity. (Leonardo da Vinci's *The Last Supper* also has considerable form via the academic charge of artistic inexactness.)

Down the decades I have been fortunate to be overwhelmed by art – for example, a room full of Rembrandt's self-portraits at "the Met" in New York, liquid light shining from nothing, to paraphrase a line from a past poem of mine. Clive James in *Play All*, his witty critique of box-set dramas, regards Rembrandt as the inventor of the close-up.

A later self-portrait exponent was Van Gogh, but it was his 1885 *Still Life with Open Bible* at the Rijksmuseum in Amsterdam that, in turn, stilled me when I studied it while on a performing trip to the Netherlands some years ago. In the painting the Bible is open at Isaiah 53, which contains the Messianic prophecy "He was despised and rejected of men; a man of sorrows, and acquainted with grief". The text, although not legible, has a dull glow: a fixed-presence metaphor. Perhaps the indistinct print replaced Van Gogh's former missionary zeal and certainty. A smaller, contemporary book also features at the base of the Bible: Émile Zola's *La Joie de vivre*. Is this a painter's parable? Ancient and Modern vying for prominence? Significant symbols representing the painter's "then and now"?

Given that this plaintive work was produced only three years before Van Gogh's self-mutilation and incarceration in an asylum, the painting becomes "story" – maybe a reflection on and foretaste of tragedy, juxtaposed with the blurred memory of former ecstasy, when religious conviction was his solace. The approaching doom was finally realized when he shot himself in the chest in July 1890, delivering dear Vincent out of the vortex of suffering.

The artists and artworks so far could be listed under the heading "masters": formal in form, technically absorbing, surprising and innovative but recognizable in their composition and representation.

As someone given to frequent attacks of random curiosity and a thirst for knowledge, I keenly attended an exhibition of the Abstract Expressionists in London in the autumn of 2016. These Shelley-like dissenters, at the experimental end of the artistic spectrum, are still, in some circles, regarded as the shock troops of the palette. The more conservative critics are sniffy and even dismissive of these free-form practitioners. The works featured at the Royal Academy of Arts by Jackson Pollock, Willem de Kooning, Mark Rothko, Lee Krasner, and others resulted in the poem concluding this chapter. The Royal Academy viewing continued my interest in this group, first flinted in the Met back in the 1980s.

The term "Abstract Expressionism" was initially used by the writer and left-field novelist Robert Coates in an article in *The*

New Yorker in 1946 as a means to describe a loose collective of post-war, resident American artists and sculptors who ditched the recognizable for the mainly abstract, in so doing becoming caricatured as the "blob and squiggle brigade".

Just as much as Fournier, Rembrandt, Van Gogh, Turner, Vermeer, and many other twenty-four carat catalogue stars have influenced and inspired me to become a lay student of art (one who has never graduated), the visceral effect of the Abstract Expressionists has caused me over the years to seek to understand the perceptions, gestures, contrasting squares and sprawls, and "shape speech" of their work.

This is so much so that the cover of my 1989 poetry collection, *A Giant's Scrapbook*, published by Hodder & Stoughton, leads with Hans Hofmann's *Pompeii*, a lavish feast of red, yellow, black, washed blue, green, and purple, a paperback coat of many colours. German-born Hofmann (1880–1966) was by 1941 an American citizen, having wised up to the fact that Hitler took his role as a deranged cultural and ethnic critic to death-camp levels: woe betide the producer of the decadent, unorthodox canvas in his narcotic presence, the one-time art student's preference being for comforting scenes of folk-tale Bavaria or an Aryan Madonna and Christ child flanked by admiring daisies. Hofmann, a pivotal influence on the new movement, having tutored Lee Krasner, wife of Jackson Pollock, brought a European sensibility to his New York classes, having mixed with Matisse and Picasso in Paris in the early years of the twentieth century.

The "Ab-Exes" brushstroke stories and coded patterns are, for me, not merely a clashing mash-up of hues and dyes, an explosion in a paint factory, but an invitation, a beckoning to let the imagination fly – admittedly not initially on any defined flight path.

Whichever way a human being seeks to express themselves, in art, dance, song, et al, they are, in that moment, consciously or unconsciously, immersing themselves in the divine pursuit of creativity, a process and a need open to all. Not an indulgence but a requirement, almost a commandment, as the Scripture-literate, songwriter-sage Leonard Cohen puts it, "to self-investigate". The serious artist is rarely a tidy character but rather an explorer of the within and the without for the benefit of all.

Like the old masters, the Abstract Impressionists are telling their stories for our benefit. Whether we choose to listen is… our choice.

"TRAGEDY, ECSTASY, DOOM"[1]

In the cloistral gallery the Abstract Expressionists
are showing us our noise, our seasons, our nightfall.
In this present we are ageing
before their tones and orchestrations,
their washes and layers,
their pigment moods; their splashed quadrangles
and smeared rectangles.

Within these mortal Post-it notes
are women, elation and yowls,
reminding us we are a census of sunsets
before the final West.
Paint as praise, fervour… and keening.

---

[1] The description by the painter Mark Rothko (1903–1970) of his, in the words of the curator of the Royal Academy exhibition, David Anfam, "perennial quest to formulate abstract embodiments of powerful human feelings".

3

BREAKAGES

The poem encountered at the end of this chapter is, in part, about the "breakages" in life that we endure, and our subsequent response to such emotional fractures, constraints, and the inevitable appointment in mortality's diary.

In October 2009, six months before his death from cancer, the one-time Sex Pistols manager, cultural saboteur, absentee art student, and bizarrely, former apprentice wine taster Malcolm McLaren gave what turned out to be his last public thoughts at the Handheld Learning conference in London. In tone it was a secular sermon, a solemn assessment of our commodified culture.

The years since that talk have not diminished nor aged the piquancy of his views – rather, they seem now like enduring prophecy. McLaren looked back to his cups, his Year Zero to 1975, when as a polymath Pied Piper he began to attract the adolescent, disaffected tribes of South London and from the post-war council estates of Kent on to his manor, the more scuffed end of the King's Road in Chelsea.

Through the propagation of "the cult of the amateur" – that is, punk and its anti-fashion fashion – McLaren pulled things apart, literally. His perverse hive was the shop, starting as Let It Rock, then called Too Fast To Live, Too Young To Die, which begat SEX, and continued into its dotage as Seditionaries. As SEX (apologies for the second name-check but that's how it was, in pink foam rubber capital letters), racks (how conventional) of ripped tee shirts, some with sweary and obscene motifs, and legs-chained-together bondage trousers were de rigueur. If you were fearless enough to mix and match and chose to wear the latter with a pair of faux leopard skin stilettos and a heavy lavatory chain necklace, when running for a train back to Bromley you'd end up with a bruised chest, a hernia, and a sprained ankle.

Together with designer Vivienne Westwood, the pair's disruptive spirits were critiquing what McLaren described as "the culture of deception". And so their foot soldiers of clothes, body jewellery, and the associated aggressive, nihilistic, head-hurting music – "three minute rackets" – coagulated into a blitzkrieg against the prevailing laissez-faire, free-market smugness.

Back then my wife Carol and I were living on the World's End estate on the King's Road opposite the former vintage clothing/high-end hippy fashion emporium Granny Takes a Trip, a few hundred yards from McLaren and Westwood's flipside enterprise. On Saturday afternoons during the scorching, safety-pin summer of '76, we were at home to "this other England", both congregation and swarm, promenading through Chelsea, revelling in their mayhem appearance and colonizing the Roebuck, a squalid hostelry overseen by the one-eyed mine host, "Fat Jack".

Consider this. Following the seizure of the Winter Palace in Saint Petersburg in October 1917, the Soviet Council of People's Commissars, headed by Lenin, issued transforming, revolutionary edicts. Sixty years later, the fomenting of insurrection in SW3 and SW10 mainly consisted of dentally challenged adolescents expectorating in the direction of frail, old soldiers wearing regimental ties. The "fascist regime", excitedly denounced in a Sex Pistols' lyric, remained intact – jackboots not required, just a spit-and-polished brogue gliding through Fortnum & Mason: a sign of the old order going about its discreet and polite business.

However, McLaren's subversion of "the Man" was progressing with barrow-boy savvy when, as Sex Pistols Svengali, he wangled two hefty record company advances from both EMI and A&M, £50,000 and £75,000 correspondingly.

McLaren – sardonic, shrewd, and manipulative – sold his band on the basis that they were unmarketable to the commercial mainstream, which they were. Having paid up, EMI then terminated the contract. The signing to "sucker number two" A&M in 1977 was staged outside Buckingham Palace, where his surly charges, as if on cue, verbally abused the Royal Family before Fleet Street's copy-grateful magpies. As Sir Richard Branson, a more well-mannered alternative entrepreneur (who later signed the Pistols to his own Virgin Records), remarked, "They had earned £125,000 for doing nothing more than a bit of swearing and vomiting and one single." Yet for McLaren this was an exercise in exposing the more venal aspects of the music business. He had picked their corporate pockets in broad daylight with quite a crowd watching and waltzed away with what he regarded as the establishment's ill-gotten loot, the deceivers deceived.

Over thirty years later before an audience of educationalists at the Barbican, pensive, concerned, and in a sedate grey jumper, Malcolm McLaren, at the age of sixty-three, invited his hearers to still see the arts and commerce as a polemical battlefield. Turning his fire on the present day "cool to be stupid" culture, he identified the warring forces as "karaoke versus authentic".

Labelling Tony Blair "a buffoon" for propagating the New Labour snakebite of "Cool Britannia", McLaren went on to give both barrels to the tyranny of the Simon Cowell School of Talent Shows, where you can put a dog on a tightrope, or vocally emote and warble your way to momentary fame. On this narcissistic catwalk, McLaren argued, everything is for sale, and the self-improving aesthetic of applied learning, the "noble pursuit of creativity", ends up swamped by the shallow and the coarse: television, technology, and the record business serving as Macbeth's three witches, invoking the shiny Satan of consumerism. McLaren's premise was "we are all in its power but don't have to be".

And yet in this weeping arcade, this culture in ruins, McLaren said he could detect an altogether different tune, "a ruby in a field of tin", singing of an ever-growing nostalgic, undeniable, and unquenchable search for authenticity across all generations and ethnicities worldwide.

If wisdom is an apprenticeship, and just when you think you may have learned something to pass on only to end up exiting this present classroom, then McLaren in his final days was passing on contemplations from his own book of Ecclesiastes, with a bit of mea culpa thrown in.

He rightly pinpointed the precision function of authentic, struggled-over art, that "messy process of creativity", with its ability to transfix and even transform both practitioner and recipient if the art itself, like the planets, is in the right alignment.

Bob Dylan wrote in the first volume of his "slow train coming" autobiography, *Chronicles*, of the imbibing effect authentic artists have had on him. Describing the "beautiful horn" voice of Hank Williams, Dylan writes in adoration, "When I hear Hank sing, all movement ceases. The slightest whisper seems sacrilege." Dylan describes that moment when art recruits and anoints you, and you can't go back to how you were – you must go on into the Pentecost of the unknown. Credible art is about simile and metaphor, be it in word or image, the search for truth, for authenticity. "The kingdom of heaven is like… is like… is like…" as one example of authentic, reported speech puts it.

So the artist who is seeking to serve their community, and not just themselves, has to learn their craft, serve their apprenticeship with rigour and in failure. The esteemed Irish poet Paul Durcan said that the great enemy of art is the ego and that ego needs to disappear so that the, in this case, poet becomes the representative of ordinary people walking past in the street.

The maternity ward for art is the imagination. As I wrote once in a poem, "imagine no imagination… hard to imagine…" but the imagination is where creativity breathes and becomes. To quote author and broadcaster Brian Sibley, the fruits of the imagination are "borne out of the author's state of unknowing" – and, as such, art materializes through a seemingly goalless orientation to produce the poems, books, songs, and paintings we crown as "authentic", the resonance of recognition.

When Lucy went through the back of the wardrobe into Narnia, the first creature she met was an other-world fawn carrying a brolly and loaded with parcels. Through *The Chronicles of Narnia*, C. S. Lewis's imagination leads him, and us, into an arresting child's fantasy adventure where metaphysics drives a narrative that considers the essence and the quality of the soul. All of this is examined and fought over in the company of the pure presence of the sacrificial Aslan.

Significant artistic movements usually have a salon in which to meet and swap imaginings. The Eagle and Child pub in Oxford where Lewis, J. R. R. Tolkien, Charles Williams, and others used to gather for smoky, rigorous debate (and at times unarmed verbal combat) was a nursery of ideas for the Narnia tales, and knowing a little about Lewis's life we could speculate that perhaps what brought such an epic tale into being was Lewis's state of perplexity at what he saw in wider society during his time; his stories emanated through conscience via imagination.

Art does not come about exclusively through quiet meditation, although that is part of the process, but perhaps it's more the intuitive response to perceived degrees of ruin that we see in *our* times, bringing us back to Malcolm McLaren's point.

Over the years, I have endeavoured to produce my authentic own – the poem "Breakages" is an attempt at such. As for the conscious occasion when I was persuaded by the first of many authentic voices? Well, maybe my Bob Dylan/Hank Williams moment was when I first heard Dylan Thomas read a poem on the BBC Home Service well over fifty years ago. Later, adolescent clarification of which poem it was identified it as "And Death Shall Have No Dominion". At the time I was smitten, and I didn't have a clue as to what he was on about. I was only seven, and up until then my big hero had been Lenny the Lion.

But oh that "honeyed baritone", Anglo–Welsh, assured voice urging, "Break in the sun till the sun breaks down…" In a small room on my pumice-stone planet[2] of Anfield, the wireless burst with bells, and to repeat Bob Dylan, all movement ceased. Unconsciously, the poetic commissioning had begun, Thomas the repetitive recruiting officer, by way of Paul's Epistle to the Romans, borrowing his poem's title from the second part of Romans 6:9.

A female fan once wrote to Thomas, and remarkably he replied (correspondence was never his strong point, especially if it was the Inland Revenue shouting through the letterbox). The woman said that she loved his poetry but was worried that her understanding of the verse may not be that which Thomas originally intended. Thomas's reply to her was that poetry was like a city, with many entrances.

It is the poet's job to faithfully record the entrances and exits, profit and loss of the human condition. In a 2009 article in *The Sunday Times*, the late cultural critic A. A. Gill, recognizing that poetry had become the way we confront mortality, described poetry as "the apex of culture, the spire of civilisations. It is the scalpel of emotion and the anvil of thought. It whispers and it bellows the unsayable with mere words." He concluded, "We tell poems to God and call them prayers."

---

[2] "Pumice-stone planet" is a parochial metaphor recalling when pre- and post-war, working-class Northern "housewives" used to remove dirt from their front steps by scraping them with an abrasive pumice stone and then scrubbing them with a brush and hot water. This was a weekly ritual my mother and grandmother carried out. Filed under "house proud", it was noticed if you didn't! Oh, the tyranny of "respectability".

BREAKAGES

We will be broken by many things;
through fierce and forced intrusions around us,
and our own wrecking ball within.
Our city walls breached,
our wings stuck and skin slicked
by insidious spillage.

We will be broken by many things;
our inherited condemnations
and judge and jury sentence.
We will be broken by events and loss;
the diagnosis and gaunt treatments,
the playground… and waiting room of remission;
the riots of grief, and the frozen days that follow.

We will be broken by many things;
the snapped promises and the "not heard" seasons,
the infringements and trespasses against us –
our violated times.
We will be broken by many things;
the soul appearing lost
through cunning and blatant conspiracies –
and our own collusions,
our sabotage, our dark matter.

We will be broken by many things…
and yet, these fractures and fragmentations
do contain waiting seeds and thorough songs.
For, we can bloom… and rise…
and rebel a new anthem;
a Midwinter chant, a Spring shanty,
a Sabbath Requiem for what was, but no more.
We no longer tarred or tethered
but transformed by
the Myriad of Light
the First-Born Broken
the original Renaissance
the only Reformation,
who in turn breaks the many things
that now break us.

4

ANFIELD, WINTER – 1960

How the poem featured at the end of this chapter came about is the result of the exploration of memory: an excavation of the intricate layers of both the conscious and subconscious; the acute recollection leading to the mining of the amnesiac past which hasn't been forgotten at all but "stored"; the hearing again or anew of the lost chords of childhood with its nectarous, and sometimes astringent, songs.

That process is, for me, brilliantly evoked by songwriter Mary Chapin Carpenter in her bone-china delicate song "Only a Dream", in which she observes her growing self in an Eden-like relationship with her sister. The image-memories are wistful, piercing, and elusive; highlighting the clarity and limbo that comes with trying to elicit an idyllic period and yet not always being able to. In her trance-state references, recalling an almost observable land of summer and showers, Carpenter opens a sensory and mystical scrapbook.

In particular, her use of the word "screen" in the song, a necessary addition to many American houses warding off squadrons of mosquitoes, summons up a sense of specific place. That word enforces a telling and true retention as we join her in a long-ago house staring through the bug-barrier gauze. For memory entails the geography of childhood – where we were, what surrounded us, and what that place emotes in us from the theatre of our past.

The author and theologian Frederick Buechner writes in *Telling Secrets* that in the constructive act of remembering, "at the farthest reach... there is peace. The secret place of the Most High is there.... the still waters, the green pastures. Home is there."

And so to "Anfield, Winter – 1960", where maritime symbolism, the foreboding houses of post-war Liverpool, the Holocaust, and my primary school coexist in a slow-tracking shot of reminiscence and "stored" rediscovery.

When I left my grammar school in 1969, I was, vocationally, all at sea. While poetry, the devouring and writing of, was becoming a constant, I hadn't yet mastered the strategy of how to make enough from Thomas's "craft or sullen art" in order to dutifully pay my widowed mother for food and lodging, plus the necessary bureaucracy of my weekly National Insurance stamp. There was also the parental instruction to put something aside in my Post Office book should I, anytime soon, move into the super tax bracket.

A few months down the meandering path and for want of anything more focused to pursue, I was taken in by the largest Unemployment Benefit Office in the city centre, the cavernous Renshaw Hall on Renshaw Street. (Renshaw Hall also followed an unsettled employment path. Starting off as a skating rink in 1909, it was barely two years in that job. Then it decided to be a parcel sorting office. Jacking that in, it became a dance hall, to be then called up for King and country as a recruiting centre during the war. It finally closed its doors to benefit claimants in 1984.)

Following my appointment as a rookie clerical assistant, and after instruction in the legislation of the National Insurance Act, I was despatched on a regular basis down to Mann Island by the Pier Head, and the Merchant Navy Establishment Office. Mann Island was a free-spirited, "resting" cabin-cum-minimal treasure chest where Liverpool's merchant seamen signed on, between voyages, to collect their hard-earned dole money and have their all-important National Insurance Card stamped and credited.

This was a heady location and environment in which to work and observe. Outside, the River Mersey shimmered and swayed, welcoming trading ships from the Americas, Africa, and the Far East, overlooked by the waterfront's architectural family jewels, the so-called Three Graces: the Royal Liver Building, completed in 1911; the baby of the trio, the Cunard Building, finished during the First World War; and the Mersey Docks and Harbour Board Building, domed and done by 1907.

Inside the cramped offices manned by a staff of five, engineers, chefs, welders, able and ordinary seamen formed, usually, an orderly crew, and sometimes spoke at the counter of their latest adventures but never graphically as there were ladies within earshot. Many bore their smudged blue forearm portraits of anchors, imagined sea serpents, and wives' and girlfriends' names. This was before the tattoo became commonplace body art. For the merchant seaman it was a sign of "adventurer", even though the inking parlours of Accra back then had a limited variety of design options.

It must be said at this point that Liverpool's commercial wealth was accrued, in part and substantially, by means of the slave trade. Following the cessation of this vile blight, these transformed former misery routes and further expansion into new seas became, admittedly, prosperous passages for these late-sixties Scousers. This is something that cannot be neatly squared; there is nothing fair about how all this twentieth-century business evolved. "There is no such thing as clean money," as the late Rabbi Hugo Gryn, an exemplary broadcaster and Auschwitz survivor, once speculated during Channel 4's *After Hours*, the engrossing, sprawling late-night discussion programme.

If I were to take you today (or next Tuesday if that suits) to my former place of employment, I could only point to its small footprint. The building no longer exists. Roughly(ish) in its place is the new Museum of Liverpool. But this is where memory does not fail or embellish or obfuscate. For me, my dead civil service colleagues and swaggering waterboys, it is the lucid fact, and not fiction, of "once upon a time".

A sizeable number of Liverpool families of the pre- and post-war era could include a number of merchant seamen either present, or sailing away from the Christmas dinner table. My maternal grandfather enrolled as a steward from the early 1900s onward. His brother, Billy, rolled down the gangplank, jumped ship in New York, and wrote occasional "made it in show business" letters home. Accurate and apocryphal stories fill Merseyside family lore: Liverpool seamen bringing home monkeys, macaws, and vaguely identified creatures to take up residence in the coal shed or enjoy an evening of yarns, squawking and screeching in the mid-nineteenth-century maritime hostelry The Baltic Fleet, across the road from the Albert Dock.

However, in a few years these men would see their working lives erased, many experiencing permanent shore leave. It was approaching the end of empire down at Mann Island. The decline in traditional merchant shipping was set with the introduction of containerization, and with drastic changes in the transporting of goods, all of these elements contributed to the discarding of the collective kitbag.

By the year 2000, a change in UK tax laws further discouraged shipping companies from using the port for these purposes.

Meanwhile, back in Anfield, with the poem's seafaring allusions rooted, my Jewish dentist and my father's never-spoken-about, gallant and traumatic war service join the picture. The final verse, where Anfield Road County Primary races through its own gates, well – that is most curious. I started writing "Anfield…" in a late-summer 2015 workshop entitled "I Remember", organized by the Poetry Society in conjunction with the Freud Museum and skilfully led by the poet Kathryn Maris, very much a "lightly-held reins" enabler. I hadn't been to a communal writing workshop for decades but I was and am intrigued with the citadels and deserts of memory. Could it be the age I am now that attracted me? The frequent misplacing of things and people…?

As I began to make notes in the workshop location, the Anna Freud Centre in Hampstead, I wrote the word "wigwam" in the margin of my notepad. How strange. A few years prior to this pivotal workshop exercise, I had had an amiable email exchange with author and stand-up comic Alexei Sayle, a fellow pupil at the Anfield Road County Primary. I had used a clip of a radio programme Alexei had made for BBC Radio 4, *Alexei at the Seaside with the Unions*, during my regular duties as writer and presenter on *Pick of the Week* for the same network.

Alexei thanked me for using the extract and asked if I remembered anything of our school days, boys' names or particular teachers, and had we carried on with our needlepoint studies? That sort of thing. This pleasantly nostalgic chit-chat took place when Alexei was launching the first volume of his autobiography, *Stalin Ate My Homework*. He and I had had no contact since our school years and our brief encounters I seem to remember only ever took place at playtime on account of me being in a different gang of one.

In his very funny and plaintive journal of his Anfield upbringing, Alexei referred to a sandpit… and a *wigwam* in the grounds of our alma mater. Well, as the saying should go, you could have knocked me down with a Native American chief's headdress. I had "stored" the memory of the wigwam deep in a mental cave where the cavalry couldn't find it, and I'd consigned it to its shadowed oblivion. Why a wigwam was in the playground, I couldn't say; perhaps in anticipation of an impending powwow between Sioux elders, camped at nearby Fazakerley, and squat urchins in balaclavas, who wouldn't be allowed to inhale a peace pipe. But it was Alexei's reaching back to that time reviving a permanent red and yellow antecedent that completed the poem.

After some necessary editing and amending, workshop leader Kathryn then invited me to read the poem (along with

chosen fellow attendees) as part of The Creative Unconscious –
Psychoanalytic Poetry Festival during the early autumn of 2015,
where poet Annie Freud, a daughter of the painter Lucian Freud
and great-granddaughter of Sigmund Freud, performed some of
her moving work.

Allowing for memory, that is as complete a narrative I can give
regarding the genesis and development of the following poem…
for now, anyway. As Oscar Wilde perceived, "Memory… is the
diary that we all carry about with us." Sometimes we forget where
that diary is, then on discovery add more… because memory is
both fixed and transient, and yet still in progress, depending on
what it is we are remembering.

ANFIELD, WINTER – 1960

The ghost houses and spectral villas sigh.
A parrot blinks in a late afternoon parlour,
an old sea bird on permanent shore leave
with salty language and a botched tattoo.

He has no horizon now.
Perched on his closed trunk,
full of pecked postcards of Lagos
and the Gold Coast,
he tastes warm sea winds.

Over the road the dentist's chair leans back,
a mid-air, slow, fainting;
his drill as thick as a capstan.
He applies gas; the mask is thick rubber crude.
How did he know how much to give
to an eight-year-old without killing him?

And did he freeze each time he did this –
remembering his perished own?

My father had seen such things. Came home,
kept schtum, had nightmares, carried on living…
… and died.

Further along the road
school classrooms are clogged empty.
The inkwells, a drought of arid blue lagoons.
The bell tower, quiet as rust,
a brick Matterhorn of consciousness.
The playground, blank in mist
with its phantom wigwam,
a child's attraction
which I was too fearful to enter.
Apart from just now
when I began to remember some of this.

5

UNDER THE CLOCK

A suburban Liverpool cinema, now demolished; a book recommendation from a television producer; and a BBC Radio 4 documentary I presented in the summer of 1999 about the double Oscar-winning British cinematographer Jack Cardiff – all of these contributed to the toe-tapping "performance" poem "Under the Clock", the main feature at the end of this chapter.

Even following that radio programme encounter with the auteur Cardiff, whom Martin Scorsese cites as a primary influence on his work, my poem continued to be "in production" and took several more years to sail into harbour. Most poets and writers however would probably say no piece of work finally "docks" but that it will do for now, often to reappear later wearing different verbal patterns, and even amendments.

Like film and theatre, poetry creates, among other attributes, landscapes of ideas, prospects, and sketches of, and from, the imagination. One listener likened my performance to "verbal video". To continue with the filmic vocabulary, my awakening to making "movies of the mind" began in earnest at the Carlton Cinema in the Tuebrook district of Liverpool from the mid-1960s onward. Pre- and post-war Liverpool gleamed with a galaxy of Gaumonts, Hippodromes, Astorias, and Anfield's uniquely monikered Cabbage Hall Picture House. But the brick-built Carlton (once the city's largest cinema) was my gravitational pull.

Opened in the early summer of 1932, the Carlton was nigh on a 2,000-seater cinematic cavern with distinctive design features such as bounding stags on the walls, wing motifs, and atmospheric low lighting: a grotto of mute gold in which to settle and be anointed by a screen rainbow.

Being different times then, smoking was expected; smoke sauntering in the projector's beam, it added secular incense to the contemplative experience. And (note to young people) there were certainly none of those small skips of popcorn you get nowadays on offer in the kiosk foyer. Just boxes of Maltesers ("nothing pleases like…"), packets of Opal Fruits ("made to make your mouth water"), and the latest ABC Film Review – a thumping good read at sixpence a pop, which you couldn't peruse in the dark, obviously.

As a solitary attendee content in my own company, I became enthralled by the ruminative presence of Paul Scofield as Sir Thomas More in Robert Bolt's *A Man for All Seasons*; I was further stirred by the pleasingly odd mood-music soundtrack of Ennio Morricone in *The Good, the Bad and the Ugly,* which made yodelling and whistling intoxicatingly cool. Sadly, in England's World Cup-winning year, the facial bristles of Clint Eastwood failed to win the Oscar for Best Supporting Stubble, but romantic cliché as broad-brush archetype prevailed. Having shot quite a lot of people without asking if they'd mind, the anti-hero-hero (hero minus?) rode off wearing an outlaw poncho, a garment I have never been able to carry off without attracting some ill-mannered guffawing from people who share the present household.

Back to the future – the Carlton hits kept coming: Stanley Kubrick's *2001: A Space Odyssey* with screenplay co-written by Arthur C. Clarke; Neil Simon's outstanding *The Odd Couple,* where comedy begets tragedy becoming inverse fellowship by way of Jack Lemmon and Walter Matthau's supreme acting. This cemented my devotion to musicals, and show tunes, with the deft lyric; for example, Barbra Streisand in *Hello, Dolly!,* a sovereign artist who could make "Nellie the Elephant" sound like a breast-heaving torch song.

On reflection, what I was imbibing through this motion picture ad hoc apprenticeship was the alchemy of the disparate elements of film, which, in turn, began to animate my own rough, fledgling poetry. The best films are the visual exploration of aspects of the human condition, the mortal coil to which we are all subject. For me two paramount examples of such are Martin Scorsese's 1980 boxing epic, *Raging Bull*, and Michael Powell and Emeric Pressburger's immediate post-war allegory, *A Matter of Life and Death*. The cinematographer on the latter was Jack Cardiff, whose talents Scorsese described as "the lens as brush strokes… a true pioneer of colour".

I have Jonathan Mayo to thank for piquing my initial interest in Jack Cardiff. Jonathan was my trusted location producer/director for a television series (several as it turned out) we both worked on in the late 1990s, based at the BBC in Manchester. Both of us have a fan's interest in all things popular culture, especially film-related. One evening while I was staying with him, Jonathan asked if I'd come across a book called *The Prince, the Showgirl and Me: The Colin Clark Diaries*. My response was that I hadn't, but now caught in the slipstream of Jonathan's enthusiasm I was very much intrigued, and in particular by the mention of one Jack Cardiff, cinematographer on the film *The Prince and the Showgirl*, referred to in the diary.

The book was the first volume (there were two in total) and gave Colin Clark's account of when, as a well-connected, with requisite Old-Etonian charm, twenty-three-year-old third assistant director – that is, runner-cum-minder – he became factotum on- and off-set to the actor and director, as well as producer, Sir Laurence Olivier. Reflecting many years later when I interviewed him, Colin Clark fulsomely credited Jack Cardiff with not only making Marilyn Monroe, Olivier's co-star, shimmer on camera but also for saving the film itself from imploding. I was to be a privileged party to this rare combination of artistry and diplomacy when I eventually came to interview Jack Cardiff for the Radio 4 documentary *Jack Cardiff Speaks*.

In a "hair-in-the-gate" summing up, the megastars of the film – the grand theatrical knight and the brittle queen of Hollywood – were not complementary supernovas but different, clashing solar systems. The English repertory-trained Olivier, meticulous in preparation and discipline, expected Monroe, the studio-reared asset, to turn up, hit her mark, and know her lines backward – but preferably forward.

This was not to be. Monroe's psychological frailty, extremely wayward timekeeping, reliance on method-acting coach Paula Strasberg for direction (thus usurping Olivier), and the developing tensions in her marriage to her own intellectual prince, American playwright Arthur Miller, made for a noxious, explosive atmosphere at Pinewood. With Olivier increasingly at snapping point, Colin Clark, as a mediator between Olivier, Monroe's "people", and the star herself, and Jack Cardiff, tact in full-focus, turned the film from a destructive brood-fest to light comedy sparkle. A remarkable salvage mission really, given Olivier's scathing descriptions of his fellow actor's disintegrating personality. Five years after the film's release in 1957, Marilyn Monroe was found dead in her Los Angeles home. The speculation as to the precise cause of death continues to this day.

Equipped with further research into the career of Jack Cardiff and sure, as one can be, that this would make a late-morning scheduled half-hour feature for Radio 4, I wrote up a treatment and took the idea to David Prest, former in-house Radio 4 features producer and then, as now, MD of the radio independent Whistledown Productions.

My association with David went back to the early 1990s, when as producer of *Going Places* he invited me to have a go at some features for that jolly and much-missed Friday evening programme.

David took the programme idea to Radio 4, who quickly gave it a clapperboard "yes". We set about assembling our cast list of interviewees: colleagues who had worked with Jack or had knowledge of his superlative technical accomplishments, including John Box, production designer on the previously mentioned *A Man for All Seasons, Lawrence of Arabia,* and *Doctor Zhivago.* Eva Monley was also tracked down; she had been location scout and production assistant on *The African Queen*, which was filmed by Jack Cardiff in Uganda, what was then the Belgian Congo and in Isleworth Studios, and featured the mighty talents of Katharine Hepburn and Humphrey Bogart.

And so on an early summer's day, six months prior to the millennium, David and I entered the stone-floor kitchen of Jack's eighteenth-century Grade II-listed townhouse in the centre of Saffron Walden to be overwhelmed, certainly in my case, by a photographic gallery of Hollywood's royal women – stunning stills emphasizing Jack's lighting genius, a luminous salon of beauty and eminence: Ava Gardner, Ingrid Bergman, Audrey Hepburn, Marlene Dietrich, and possibly the most ephemeral and, paradoxically, eternal of them all, Marilyn Monroe.

We retired to the drawing room, where paintings by Jack in the manner of the various greats, Vermeer, the French Impressionists such as Renoir, and others graced the walls. Over the course of a two-hour interview, Jack gave insights into his art – "the best kind of light is natural light" – from the award highs to the can-kicking lows of his career. There was his Oscar for *Black Narcissus* in 1947 – the ultimate gold star – which Jack generously allowed me to cradle. But then there was the inexplicable studio rejection of *The Red Shoes*, now hailed as one of the greatest films ever. J. Arthur Rank walked out of the viewing room in silence, refusing it a premiere. The film was then exiled to the post-war art houses of New York, where, in 1948, an infant Martin Scorsese sat with his father to be astounded by "the movie that plays in my heart".

One film that absorbed me and which we talked about at length was *A Matter of Life and Death*, starring David Niven and Kim Hunter. It was made just after the war, one of the four films Jack made with the directors and writers Michael Powell and Emeric Pressburger. I found, and still find, "the metaphysical melodrama set halfway between earth and heaven" (to quote film historian Professor Ian Christie) hypnotic, especially the juxtaposition of the heaven scenes, in monochrome, against the back-on-earth-scenes in intoxicating technicolour.

In the film David Niven plays an RAF pilot, Peter Carter, who bails out of his burning plane over the English Channel. Due to a clerical error, foppish angel Marius Goring makes a pig's ear of his task of accompanying the crashed airman onto the everlasting landing runway. As Carter is going down, he begins to fall in love with his land-based radio operator, Kim Hunter. Although helpless to save him, she becomes his beacon of hope before he "buys it" because, as the film affirms, "nothing is stronger than love". Meanwhile in the continuous heavenlies, between space and time, a celestial court deliberates the combatant's fate. Should it be now or later that he's enrolled into the afterlife?

Bearing in mind when the film was made, the poignant scenes of allied airmen – American, French, British, and Commonwealth – arriving, they're not sure where, to be "registered in the air crew section" and allotted their "ultimate wings" becomes a sensitive and salient metaphor about "when all this is over…". And it was those pertinent imaginings that gave "Under the Clock" *its* consideration of wings: an earth-bound deliberation, which for now "knows not… [but] through a glass, darkly". For, what lies beyond remains opaque and elusive. Yet, one day hence…?

UNDER THE CLOCK

We're all under the clock
the mortal tick-tock
with a limit of days
'til we finally dock
We're all under the clock
You, me, Mr Spock,
at the final frontier
where the soul is unlocked…
we the copious masses
awaiting our passes

there'll be chain mail rappers,
nuns and slappers,
the celibate, the horny
who've gone at it like the clappers,
the lowly and the emperor,
the Chihuahua with distemper,
the pacifists and therapists
who hid their raging temper,
the changing guards, addictive bards
and radio presenters
and tiny curled babies
still attached to their placentas,
the meek, the sleek, the Jew, the Greek,
the Muslim, Hindu and the Sikh…
the proud employee of the week

We're all under the clock
the mortal tick-tock
with a limit of days
'til we finally dock
We're all under the clock
You, me, Mr Spock,
at the final frontier
Where the soul is unlocked…
a palette of faces
all hoping for places…

… there's the posh school headmaster,
the Jah-loving Rasta,
the runner on steroids whose timings got faster,
the gay, the bi, the hetero,
the sexually confused,
the shy, the sly, the panto dame, the achingly abused,
the terrorists on scholarships –
their bomb successfully fused…

… the criminal, the minimal,
the short, the very tall,
the tightrope walker and the stalker
and the Albert Hall…

… the harmless and the charmless,
the cardinal, the bishop,
the guard who stroked the lips of Christ
with a stick of hyssop…

… and not forgetting the Druid
and those included in Clwyd…

We're all under the clock,
the approaching knock knock
the end of our lease
when the turmoil will cease
We're all under the clock
with time to take stock
of the treasure to take
not the forged or the fake
we're all under the clock
we're all under the clock
we're all under the clock…
tick-tock… tick-tock… tick tock…

6

BLIND DATE

The deaths in recent years of two people, both instrumental in initially bringing my poetry to a wider audience, prompted the following edited, scrapbook retrospective of the random opportunities offered during my early years' development.

Peggy Poole, who died in the summer of 2016, was, as recorded by her obituary in *The Guardian*, "an unstinting champion of emerging poets". For twenty years from 1967 to 1988, Peggy produced Radio Merseyside's literary programme *First Heard* and its later manifestation, *Write Now*. In tandem, she organized the Wirral-based poetry readings called "Jabberwocky", where I performed circa 1971. These events were "wide church" gatherings featuring local poets, but also Faber stars like Ted Hughes and Seamus Heaney. Peggy mixed and matched, taking the inclusive approach to all our benefit.

Seeing some sort of promise, Peggy kindly invited me on to the local airwaves, where I read alongside the likes of Adrian Henri, another great encourager of apprentice poets, and Matt Simpson, one of Liverpool's elder statesmen of verse. This was heady company for one starting out. Both these men, sadly, are no longer with us.

Around the same time, I began to venture into the city's pop-up poetry venues, such as the Why Not pub in Harrington Street, organized by Sylvia and Harold Hikins. The first half of the evening was given over to eager herberts such as I in "open mic" spots, although I don't remember there being a microphone. The second half was given over to more established Merseyside poets of the time, such as Sidney Hoddes, and Brian Jacques, later to find world book fame as the author of the *Redwall* series of children's novels.

The second person to line up in giving me a break was John Pac (family name – Paculabo), later to become best man at my wedding. John, who died in 2013, was a local legend as singer, songwriter, and instrumentalist in the folk band Trinity Folk, which morphed into Parchment, and a record deal with Pye.

As Anfield inhabitants, our topography stretched from John's parents' house in Newcombe Street, just around the corner from the dented-nose sophistication of the Wooky Hollow nightclub with its bulging bouncers in dicky-bows, where a fast-ailing Gene Vincent played his last ever British date in October 1971. I stayed in less exciting "Lower Anfield" on Utting Avenue in my grandmother's semi with an outside wash house and buried Anderson shelter in her tidy back garden.

One early evening (possibly in 1971), in The Old Barn off Breck Road, a snug belter of a back-street pub with a clientele of "oul fellers" (Liverpudlian parlance for gentlemen of advancing years), creamy mild on the pumps, gas masks for goalposts in the backyard, etc., John and I, forsaking the conventional attire of flat caps and mufflers, convened. We were, in contrast to the regulars, favourably attired in our Woodstock Festival-influenced garb – flares, grandad three-button coloured vests, and faux furry jackets. Unbeknownst to me we were there to discuss my future, although it wasn't exactly flagged in those career-defining terms.

Trinity Folk, comprising then of John, sublime vocalist and songwriter Sue McClellan, and banjo player and penny whistle maestro Norman Hall, were getting regular gigs. I was starting out, so John suggested I come along with the band on selected dates to read a few poems. Trinity Folk's set lists at that time consisted not only of self-penned songs but also traditional ballads, carols, and folk dirges; their experimental repertoire was on a par with other electro-traditional exponents of the time such as Steeleye Span and Fairport Convention: bands who were not only army great-coated autoharp strummers, but also woolly haired contemporary revivalists.

During this period I was hoovering up influences – from the operas of Gilbert and Sullivan through to the black American London hotel cabaret artists Layton and Johnstone. It was the writers of pre- and post-war songs who drew my feverish interest, in particular Cole Porter and Dorothy Fields. If there was a circus of words going on, I was in the front row taking it all in. Now with another stream of influence to explore, consisting of tune-tales of gothic moors, compromised maidens, and lascivious squires, my modest record collection was growing less modest.

Through the Penguin Modern Poets anthologies, writers new to me were joining my gang, including Stevie Smith, whose relationship with God involved a fair amount of persistent bickering in a keeping-one's-voice-down English kind of way. Her profoundly simple and simply profound short verses contained oceans of reticence and disapproval, a ceremonial doubter demanding fair play. Years later at a family wedding I met two of my wife Carol's relations, Michael and Anna Browne, who knew Miss Smith very well – so well that the poet from Palmers Green wrote a sweetly moving poem, prosaically titled "O Pug!", to their elderly, fragile lap dog. How thrilling – two degrees of separation from Stevie Smith. Questions ensued that afternoon in a Wiltshire garden, and later in their West London home, with the engaging Brownes answering my rambling enthusiastic interrogation with tact. They showed visible and deep affection for their not-long-deceased friend, the unsentimental, remarkable talent who produced "Not Waving but Drowning".

However, back in The Old Barn with not a marquee in sight, following John's invitation I left the pub walking on air. Well, actually I was walking on Oakfield Road past the strange shop that had dentures in the window, mentally writing a note to self: "Cull the clichés… unless you're using them in an ironic or lightly tragic way." For a short period I was even put on a modest but sustaining weekly wage, a most generous offer considering the band's finances were a few pennies flush of "bread and dripping".

We were all, back then, dependent on the long-suffering largesse of our respective parents, in my case my widowed mother. We may have lived on fresh air and chips, but this was my first experience of the nuances of artistic, closed-community dynamics. To quote the BBC music broadcaster, producer, and folk band member himself, Mark Radcliffe, "Bands are small private clubs in which peculiar rules apply, unspoken hierarchies prevail… and shared adventures are guaranteed." This proved to be a useful grounding for when I later joined other "bands", especially radio production teams.

And so off we trouped in Norman's canvas-covered, clankety Land Rover to Gateshead and Blackpool… and the Castanet Coffee Bar, Fleetwood. Sixty miles an hour tops, with the engine croaking and occasionally squawking like an overworked mangle. Trips down the M6 followed to Home Counties engagements: teacher training colleges and small concert halls where nice, polite people sat and listened appreciatively… This was the life.

Wishing to prove myself useful as a crew member, I took it upon myself to be John's sitar "minder", carrying it to and from the wagon. This distinctive musical attraction and exotic talking point, which John mastered with élan, later suffered a bash to the gourd, causing a withering split in its bulbous base. Although it wasn't me that dropped this most subtle piece of craftsmanship, the unfortunate calamity became a prophetic metaphor for the cessation of all things, mechanical or breathing … or being in a band.

Later, toward the end of my time as a grateful cast-list poet, would come the early 1970s limousine for all touring bands, a

Ford Transit. It was a hard-knock white jobbie with a pale gold stripe down each side, a somewhat mimsy gilding for what was basically a hooligan with a narky gear box: the sort of vehicle that could start a fight in an empty car park.

In time, Norman left the band. Trinity Folk became Parchment, with guitarist and vocalist Keith Rycroft joining, bringing his enriching songwriting skills as the new line-up embarked on the difficult "making it" years, whatever "it" was (and how do you know when you've arrived at "it"?).

During these years, such on-the-job training, with the obligatory clanging errors and terrors (have you ever played Cumbernauld?), taught me the essential rudiments of performance – timing, reading an audience, suitability of material for the audience, listening to an audience, varying the material… and how to go about condensing the big themes of life into a, hopefully, understandable yet sleight-of-hand, two-and-half-minute poem that leaves the desired beneficial silence on completion before the satisfying applause. As a student of comedians' techniques, I was also blotting paper absorbing these practices and prising them into my early, awkward performances, not least the delivery of the Scottish mirth master Chic Murray with his hanging silences.

Through John Pac I learned of the vast folk-ballad tradition where historical incidents, tragic love affairs, and accounts of ancient rituals are compressed into, ideally, not too many verses complete with a breezy or bleating chorus. I was becoming aware of the poetic equivalent through Tennyson, Coleridge, and the like. But how then to write "poetry that sings of true things" in obvious, not-obvious ways? Poetry that brings almost conversational relevance, in which a yearning for deliverance and ascent was conveyed while measuring the isolating depths of the pestilent caves at the same time.

In "The Birch Grove", Northern Irish poet Seamus Heaney alludes to a speech from Nobel Prize-winner, and former prisoner of conscience, Joseph Brodsky, who said: "If art teaches anything (to the artist, in the first place), it is the privateness of the human condition." As a meditative addendum to that, Heaney's compatriot Louis MacNeice, in his poem "Snow", writes of the seemingly "incompatible", of "snow and pink roses against it", and "the drunkenness of things being various".

It is *not* the poet's job to make things trim. To quote Allen Ginsberg, "Poetry is not an expression of the party line" but rather "making the private world public". Drawing on the contradictory wisdom of Heaney, Brodsky and Ginsberg, the poet can become a kind of helpmeet for the reader or listener, bringing meagre balm to people in order that they feel a little less alone.

The "things being various" poem that follows explores the many rooms one enters if on the receiving end of betrayal, and the long comprehending process, especially for introverts, about what has occurred, with its Greek chorus "of blank", and cul-de-sacs "of intense", and often raging feelings. The attempt at resolution at the end of the poem is no easy fix, but rather a hint of assuaging counsel to assist in the turning back from the whirlpool of continuous and destructive self-recrimination or devouring resentment: a hint of purging and cleansing.

King Kong, in his original 1933 version, is the metaphor employed as a symbol of betrayal and exploitation. "Let's take the big lunk to Broadway… we'll clean up… First, we'll need some really strong chains. What a dumb monkey." Kong and the "I" in the poem become an exclusive fellowship of suffering, facing up to the many emotions that rear up in the betrayed. As Emily Dickinson once wrote, "Pain has an element of blank", alongside the twin peaks of shock and measured resignation.

BLIND DATE

Lying on the sidewalk
next to the contorted King Kong,
flash bulbs like luminous blow bubbles
pop over us.

Though dissimilar, the ape and I are in
the same submerging boat.
Curiously, he has less nasal hair than me,
his tarmac black nostrils,
a bald vortex.
His closing breaths now are oceans amplified,
mine are paddling pool rasps.
Having both been strafed
our plummet was akin.
While Kong roared
and swatted at his betrayers –
taking one out,
my slow shock meant that I took
several ages to realize I'd been hit.

So here we are,
prostrate in our brief, outdoor hospice.

Both hearing the klaxon choirs
of headline sirens approaching.
Kong obviously will command more copy
in tomorrow's editions;
but before that,

each other's face is our mutual last look,
as Kong incants in his lessening jungle voice,
"Blessed are the hoodwinked
for their story will be told, eventually."

7

THIS IS HOW IT IS

It could be said that artists and entertainers are "seasonal workers": sometimes literally, for example when recalling past summer engagements in Blackpool or Clacton, or the present-day lucrative residency in Las Vegas. One could however speculate that given the nightly repetition of "the act" in such relentlessly garish surroundings as the desert, this could lead the unfortunate, well-remunerated individual to question the validity of one's existence, ceasing to believe in the transformative boon of therapy, baby hedgehogs, and custard slices.

Having said that, in a manically manufactured environment such as Las Vegas where escape from the one-arm-bandit vicissitudes of life is replaced by an actual one arm bandit, not all is surface and fantasy. Along comes Nevadan royalty, Barry Manilow, reminding his customers of a Shakespearean tragedy in the spirit of Hamlet's uncle, Claudius, "when sorrows come, they come not single spies, but in battalions". Who'd have thought it: Barry and the Bard – judicious blood brothers?

To stand up my bag-of-washing thesis I refer you to the jaunty ditty "Copacabana (At the Copa)". Allow me to give you the gist. The song tells of a violent love triangle involving showgirl Lola, protective bartender Tony, and a diamond-wearing gigolo, Rico. It doesn't end well. There's a chair-throwing punch-up; Tony gets shot, once being enough. Or, time for chin-stroking – did they both shoot each other? The text is ambiguous as to which of Lola's suitors cops it. At the end of verse two we are left with a (grammatically errant) conundrum.

By the last verse, some thirty years later, Lola has lost her gig, her man, and is drinking herself into purple dancing elephants oblivion, inconsolable in her feathers. But what happened to Rico, the ne'er-do-well who caused Tony to rush to Lola's honour? We are not told. Was he banged up? Did he employ a plausible attorney who got him off? Is the rather odious Rico now a llama farmer near Yokohama? Or *was he* the recipient of the old hot lead embalmer? For those interested in the geography of cold cases, head for Havana and ask.

Leaving that cliffhanger aside, the circumstances leading to how an artist or entertainer ends up skipping through the meadows of their buttercup moments, well – they are as variable as the July weather in Portree. The converging mathematics of artistry, person, or persons of influence taking a shine to that talent, kismet, and several arbitrary factors waiting in the wings can and do determine an artist's centre stage, transitory twinkling, or longer period of leaping in the limelight.

Conversely, all that zip-a-dee-doo-dah notoriety can evaporate when an artist falls out of favour. The freeze-frame of fate ensures their CV remains static. On frequent occasions, humiliating sackings become the bailiffs that turf a reputation out of the door. I have witnessed this in network radio, where presenters are bustled away with the fog of a press release informing the great British public of the departed's supreme talents "but it was nothing personal", all to do with the battalions of "refreshing the schedule".

If you are an artist who has found themselves in for the long haul, then "this is how it is" is the wheel-of-fortune refrain that features in the poem following these ruminations. So, which came first, the poem or this chapter? In this case, the poem… for… "this is how it is".

This knowing observation of Hollywood and Broadway actress Rosalind Russell (Tony Award winner and nominated for an Oscar on several occasions) captures the flimsiness of fame: "Flops are part of life's menu and I've never been a girl to miss out on any of the courses." Even garlanded actresses cannot be sure of longevity.

Nor can "journeyman theatricals" such as Arthur Tolcher, whom many of my generation will recall as the abject harmonica player who raced on in white tie and tails to play four bars of the "Spanish Gypsy Dance" during Morecambe and Wise's flagship telly patter, only to be banished to the wings with the catchphrase from, mainly, Eric, "Not now, Arthur." This was a running gag that ensured national fame for Arthur during the extraordinary reign of Morecambe and Wise's Saturday night shows on the BBC from 1968 to 1977. And when that gag had finally run its course, big agent spoke unto smaller agent. Arthur's contract was not renewed… "this is how it is".

Yet, as someone who has always been drawn to the story of not only the spangled star but also the less adorned bit-part player, I instigated the radio documentary that was *Not Now Arthur* to honour the Bloxwich-born turn. Having submitted the idea and following a bit of a commissioning skirmish, the light fandango was duly skipped and the programme scheduled.

So it was, on a damp day in the late spring of 2007 in Walsall Cemetery, with my producer Eleanor Thomas doing her technical finest, I recorded my closing link for the Radio 4 documentary *Not Now Arthur*.

A bemused council employee stood by. His morning task had been to find the painfully modest grave of Arthur Stone Tolcher, which he did in an accommodating spirit of "nonplusment". "Who was this feller?" our graveyard guide asked. I remember my patchy, imprecise reply: "The bloke who never got to play his harmonica on the BBC TV Morecambe and Wise shows." Nope. Recognition was still circling through dense cloud and not yet landing.

As we stood in the drizzle staring down at the small, horizontal stone plaque, I was aware that my homily, a finale of respect, was, probably, to the Metropolitan Borough attendant a thin chorus of esoteric words in the air... *As a performer Arthur Tolcher was more than the comic cowbell he carried for the latter part of his life. And if there is a Hippodrome heaven, a Palladium paradise, a Variety Valhalla where the dressing rooms are all the same size, I'd like to think that's where Arthur is now. But with all things being equal, up there he's finally top of the bill... A case of "Now... Arthur".*

The making of the programme became a diary of British wartime and post-war entertainment. Arthur had met Morecambe and Wise on the touring show *Youth Takes a Bow* in the early 1940s. Arthur and Eric shared similar ambitious mothers (the formidable Beatrice and Sadie respectively), who steered their sons' early careers, blitzing agents, promoters, and the BBC by way of, just this side of, haranguing letters. As Eric and Ernie progressed from BBC Radio comedy crosstalk spots to their later razzle-dazzle, character-defined stratosphere, courtesy of writer Eddie Braben, Arthur plodded away in end-of-an-era concert parties and pantomimes staged by Birmingham impresario Derek Salberg, with Arthur regarded as a reliable musical turn presenting a harmonica repertoire that included Ravel's "Bolero" and Gershwin's "Rhapsody in Blue".

As I interviewed people who knew and worked with Arthur Tolcher, such as Eric Morecambe's widow Joan; sixties-chart-topper Frank Ifield; actor and eminent entertainment historian Roy Hudd; and Sir Bill Cotton (who as Head of BBC Light Entertainment secured Morecambe and Wise for his Saturday night banquet schedule), Arthur emerged as a noble, fourth-on-the-bill foot soldier and supporting servant to the stars: humble and benign, a professional dependable, willing to serve the gag for the greater good of the production.

When Arthur Tolcher, a devout Catholic who never married and had a fondness for budgies and bullfights, died in March 1987, just one newspaper printed a scant obituary: the Wolverhampton *Express & Star*. During the making of the programme, one of Arthur's cousins gave me Arthur's old address book. It was a poignant little blue affair with his Equity number in the front alongside his costume measurements detailing his height and weight. There were contact phone numbers and addresses, including Eric Morecambe's listed under Eric's birth surname, Bartholomew. Cameron Mackintosh was also included, just in case the foremost West End producer had a part for a harmonica player at the defiant barricades in *Les Miserables*.

I was embarrassed, and felt uncomfortable to have this treasured personal memento of a man I'd never met, so I passed it on to Roy Hudd for his extensive memorabilia collection of British music hall and variety. Roy had, in fact, attended Arthur's funeral, following which he took possession of a bequeathed box of personal items including Arthur's unpublished memoir.

If some poems are, in part, a cri de cœur on behalf of a person or an issue that the poet notes as having gone unrecognized, then what follows is without a happy-ever-after conclusion: what Franciscan theologian and philosopher Richard Rohr identifies as "both-and". Yet the poem is also a mini charter, a broad-sweep indenture almost, for the performer, whatever their artistic discipline, as to how the business of becoming known tends to work.

Junctures of acceptance and rejection coexist. Jubilation and disheartenment are the "ugly sisters" in our shows, yet neither defines who or what we are as artists, or as human beings. The final lines of the poem *are* there for solace, but with an attempt at the bigger, redemptive vision of perspective – 360-degree seeing: a seeing that goes beyond our euphoric or disappointed selves. As *The New York Times* theatre critic, the late Brooks Atkinson advised, "The most fatal illusion is the settled point of view. Life is growth and motion"; for this, I would suggest, is how it is… but I'm not chipping that into a gravestone.

THIS IS HOW IT IS

We meet people
who give us access to others… contacts.
And this is how it is for some months,
for some fertile seasons.

Through such pollination
books are published, programmes made,
mulled wine concerts organized,
exhibitions mounted with the selective process
of who, or who not, to invite.
This is how it is.

Then when the fruit begins to drop,
remaining ungathered on the early frost grass,
and confident e-mails receive no reply
with the follow-up reminder
reading like it's been written by a wasp with a hangover
– that is the dangerous time, the void
where we cast ourselves as obsolete,
now out of season,
this is how it is.

Yet for those who hold the sway of ingress
the same will happen to them too.
Granted their memorial service
may attract more than yours,
for this is how it is.

Elsewhere, children are being scorched dead…
let it go… let it go…
this is how it is.

8

HOW CLATTER IS THE WORLD

For people of my generation, and earlier, the name Malcolm Muggeridge – journalist, satirist, and broadcaster – may now seem as distant and peculiar as a biblical prophet, a lamenting Jeremiah waving his cigarette holder stage prop on 1950s/1960s television; or perhaps a figure in a Peter Blake-like collage, in which post-war politicians, demagogues, pop stars, and cultural commentators are positioned as mannequin guests in a mock-up wedding photograph: Malcolm Muggeridge standing between box-office-bounty entertainer Alma Cogan and Gamal Abdel Nasser, the pan-Arab radical President of Egypt during the engulfing Suez Crisis 1956.

Such a juxtaposed gallery, a gathering of the unlikely, would have appealed to Muggeridge, just as when he found himself "honoured" by Madame Tussauds in 1968, his immediate waxwork companions included Twiggy, Elizabeth Taylor, and Winston Churchill's wartime ally and headache, President de Gaulle.

Malcolm once told me he looked forward to the day when he became "waxwork non grata", to be carted off and melted down. This was followed by the uninhibited laughter of true glee. For Malcolm, during his 1970s Indian-summer years, the "joke" of "all is vanity" coincided with his own empty-fortune accreditation reaching its uproarious zenith.

The incongruity of such things appealed to the dissenting, discontented Muggeridge, the kaleidoscopic span of his life being full of wild dramas of "the mishmash and bashed in": his front row view witnessing grotesque empires; private audiences with the notorious; and appearing in razzamatazz side shows.

This was the man who had taken toast and scones with an ageing Lord Alfred Douglas, Oscar Wilde's "Bosie" and petulant lynchpin in Wilde's downfall, "in a small villa in Hove", Muggeridge wrote, in a room featuring portraits of a younger, beautiful Bosie – "blazered, straw-hatted, exquisite". For all his vituperative character decimations of those he took against in a former age of deference (a long-distinguished list that included Churchill, the Royal Family, President Kennedy, and the Prime Minister at the time of Suez, Sir Anthony Eden), Malcolm's forensic eye could also hold a compassionate gaze on those he regarded as genuinely meek, non-compliant, or emotionally flailing. It was those he perceived as puffed-up, haughty, or inebriated by power that ignited Malcolm's ire. Malcolm was the hedonistic puritan heckling public life's comedy of errors.

Yet it was a late-life television encounter with a Catholic nun, Mother Teresa (who had devoted her life to alleviating the suffering of Calcutta's destitute), that led to what Malcolm regarded as all his strivings being put into a mortal and eternal perspective… and he found himself lacking, and wanting. His 1969 interview-led television documentary for the BBC, *Something Beautiful for God*, directed by Peter Chafer, has been seen as the catalyst for Malcolm's Christian conversion, although as the biography *Muggeridge*, by fellow satirist Richard Ingrams, acutely observes, Malcolm skirted with the "divine conundrum" all his adult life, dancing around the maypole of God in the contrarian, opposite direction.

In his later years when he was invited on to the long table of the British Christian establishment, Malcolm became truly ecumenical. In private, he could be equally caustic about some of the evangelical, Catholic, and Anglican leading lights he now found himself being courted by, sensing "the sin" of personal ambition and vainglorious advancement in the cloisters. However, for Malcolm, Mother Teresa became and remained the credible manifestation of Christ's radical activism as encapsulated in her lodestone verse, her mission statement, "Yet not I, but Christ liveth in me" (from the New Testament book of Galatians), when she exhorted her trainee nuns not to speak about Jesus to the suffering impoverished but to *be* Jesus to them.

My personal association with Malcolm and Kitty Muggeridge began back in 1974, in the early months of my marriage to Carol. The Muggeridges were friends of my mother-in-law, Flo Dobbie. Along with my father-in-law, she had retired to East Jerusalem. When it came to Malcolm's attention that Carol was without immediate geographical parental contact, he announced to her that he was appointing himself and Kitty as in loco parentis: not so much a suggestion, more a decree. This meant frequent trips down to Robertsbridge in Sussex from Hammersmith in West London, where we were living at the time.

Looking back, those visits were privileged private tutorials with an incisive, flawed, and self-deprecating anarchist who saw the ultimate futility in to-the-barricades revolution, and who still twinkled with, off-the-record, Fleet Street and green room gossip, sometimes displaying pantomime, comic outrage.

On one occasion, Malcolm pointed accusingly at the radiogram in the drawing room. He and Kitty listened daily, like many of their generation, to the lunchtime BBC radio news. "Dear boy," he exclaimed, "I heard the voice of Satan on that, the other day." As stand-alone statements went, this could be filed under "unsubstantiated… but riveting". Kitty, with beautiful restraint, informed us that it was not Beelzebub, as such, reading the shipping forecast, but Henry Kissinger – President Nixon's National Security Advisor, and Secretary of State – uttering a wily, statesman-like obfuscation on something or other, thus poisoning Malcolm's afternoon.

By then, Kitty and Malcolm were slowly "heading for Rome" under the kindly pastoral eye of Lord and Lady Longford, much to the bewilderment of old friends like historian A. J. P. Taylor. Malcolm, in particular, traded in his previous "The Hollow Men" persona, "… dried voices… quiet and meaningless…", and, like T. S. Eliot, contemplating on and forming a mystical relationship with God, in all his moods and beauty.

I had been previously aware of Malcolm's reputation as a regular, waspish commentator on the then Home Service's *Any Questions*, which I listened to back in the 1960s. Prior to his wireless fame, Muggeridge wore the, to him, dubious and tacky laurel of "telly turn" through his captivating, and sometimes wonderfully odd, interviews on *Panorama*, one of which was with the flamboyant Spanish surrealist Salvador Dali in 1955 and is, at the time of writing, part of the BBC Four Collection iPlayer archive.

For one night only, Britain, recently liberated from rationing, enjoyed a black-and-white bizarre, alternative music-hall double act. Malcolm asked the waxed-whiskered original, his facial hair resembling a heavily lacquered skipping rope, "How did you manage to produce those marvellous moustaches?" thereby pre-empting Caroline Aherne's Mrs Merton by some forty years with this puncturing (some would say cruel) opening question. To Muggeridge's impish, theatrically enunciated enquiry, Dali sweetly described, in his brave and intermittently impenetrable English, the rigours of moustache management.

While it may not have been a complete meeting of minds between the eminent Englishman of acidic letters and an outlandish technician who did innovative things with lobsters, it was not a taunting encounter. Throughout his libidinous, devastatingly hurtful decades, Muggeridge, conversely, took a hermit's comfort from what he perceived to be, in his anguished guilty hours, the absurd uselessness of life, often retreating into both overstatement about and profound critique of the Lost Eden of twentieth-century Western civilization. In Dali, Malcolm had found an eleven-minute playmate, and what resulted was an unlikely Tweedledum and Tweedledee, and on prime-time television – a much more ludicrous instrument in Malcolm's book than one of Dali's melting clocks.

As to when this disenchantment with humankind began, one experience in his early career is in the dock as a significant culprit. In 1932, he and Kitty (they had married in 1927) sold their wearisome "bourgeois" chattels, leaving for Moscow and the presumed workers' paradise of Stalin's Soviet Union.

Malcolm was twenty-nine years old, a rookie correspondent for the then-named *Manchester Guardian*, the influential broadsheet and mouthpiece of the Fabian Society, the socialist, intellectual collective and policy group that underpinned the Labour Party's ideals of a just society. Nationalization being the centre of its stratagem, to the Fabians the Soviet Union was the template for the new, collectivist world order.

Both Kitty and Malcolm had become close observers and disciples of this domestic socialist salon through Kitty's aunt and uncle, Sidney and Beatrice Webb. The Webbs, pioneers in the establishing of the London School of Economics, drafted major documents for the expanding movement, articulating the commandments of economic distribution. Their evangelistic pamphlets and books on political theory went some way to installing the first Labour Prime Minister, Ramsay MacDonald.

The curious – some commentators have since described it as "unnecessary" – general election of early December 1923 resulted in some mercurial mathematics, which eventually led to a short-term, as it turned out, hung parliament. Ramsay MacDonald, from the top of the fragile pole, and relying on the support of Asquith's Liberals in the House, appointed Sidney Webb as his President of the Board of Trade. This gave the new cabinet minister, and Malcolm Muggeridge's future relation by marriage, an opportunity to practise his utopian remedies on behalf of the workers, albeit for just ten months.

However, just a few years later, writing from a bone-freezing winter in Moscow, Malcolm's views on the supposed Soviet ideal of earthly paradise were causing furore at home. His articles on the deathly consequences of Stalin's agricultural five-year plan, which saw individual farms absorbed into agrarian communes brutally mismanaged by henchmen bureaucrats, were ideologically way off-message. Malcolm wrote of widespread famine, starvation, and forced labour. The "disappearing" of political opponents was revealed in time. These factual dispatches of March 1933 from the Ukraine are textbook, investigative, poking-a-stick-in-the-tiger's-eye reporting, without heed to the consequences.

Wandering about without an official permit, his sure, stark prose described "abandoned villages, neglected fields... everywhere famished". Bypassing paranoid press censorship, he sent his dispatches back to Manchester under the cover of diplomatic pouches.

Malcolm and Kitty's Soviet sojourn saw them begin as Stalinist acolytes. Their dark pilgrimage soon changed them into brave, agnostic irritants. Malcolm ended his time there as a disillusioned and withering unbeliever. The proletariat trinity of Marx, Lenin, and Stalin joined his detested rogues' gallery of "no more heroes". Heaven on earth, it turned out, was emaciated by the executioner's programme. In her 2017 book, *Red Famine*, Pulitzer Prize-winning author Anne Applebaum recorded that Stalin's grain appropriation policy in the Ukraine caused the death of over 4 million people between 1932 and 1934.

On those mid-1970s visits to Robertsbridge, our time with Malcolm and Kitty followed a set pattern. Malcolm's mornings during this period were given over to the writing of the third, but alas uncompleted, volume of his autobiography, *Chronicles of Wasted Time*.

We would arrive for an early salad lunch with meats provided for us non-vegetarians, and beer generously served just for me. Reflective conversation then rambled us all eventually into the drawing room for more of the same, and some jaw-dropping reflections, plus ordinary, as well as herbal, tea for the hosts. Then a brisk afternoon walk, an activity that Malcolm adhered to all his life, whatever the weather or terrain. Sometimes Kitty joined us, but we were always accompanied by our dogs at that time, an Irish wolfhound and Yorkshire terrier. Although not particularly a dog devotee, Malcolm enjoyed the comic contrast of the dogs' sizes, and their well-behaved ambling and skittering. Following this excursion, tea and cake would then be taken in "The Ark", Malcolm's glorious, large detached study adjacent to the main house.

Carol and I learned of some of Malcolm's notable journalistic campaigns and remarkable figures encountered. For example, during his wartime service with MI6, Malcolm became reacquainted with double agent Kim Philby at one of MI6's training establishments in St Albans. (They had previously met in Fleet Street some time before.) Philby's cover was made perfect when he was appointed head of the anti-Soviet section.

Malcolm's take on Kim Philby, who was responsible for the deaths of British agents, and others, in the field, and later buried in a Moscow cemetery with full military honours, was a counterpoint aside to the received traitor's portrait. Within a pre- and post-war historical context, Malcolm acknowledged his former colleague's treacherous deeds, speculating he, Malcolm, could have been "played" and compromised, while serving in Mozambique and Lisbon. But what Malcolm also noted was that his former colleague was a "superb administrator" and hence a highly effective civil servant for the Soviet cause: a stammering, hiding-in-plain-sight bagman, good at making lists of "things to do" as suggested by his Kremlin masters.

And then there were pithy recollections of times with Graham Greene, P. G. Wodehouse, George Orwell, all remembered in Malcolm's leader-writer detail – not smelling of rehearsed anecdotes but more spontaneous recall, with the observed quirks and idiosyncrasies of the individuals acting as further insight into their respective characters.

I didn't fully realize when I was writing this chapter's poem, "How Clatter is the World", that it has about it an essence of Malcolm. A hint of being in the stalls, taking notes. This awareness of "remote influence" came later as I typed the final version.

Malcolm was, foremost, a zealot for the authentic, a seeker after the perpetual sustenance of the soul. I pictured him, and Kitty, following their respective deaths. Malcolm went first, shambling into the afterlife with renewed, keen mind, finding nothing to criticize any more. All the personally damaging kind of dwelling on absurdity dissolved within the presence of God.

Malcolm and Kitty's generosity toward Carol and me at a pivotal time in our young lives was key. The day he put his arm around me and said, "We writers have a job to do," felt like a commissioning. Bearing in mind at that time I'd written a few twiddly, passable, but mostly inadequate poems, while Malcolm, through his past editorship of *Punch*, had served as the founding godfather of noisy objection, motivating the emerging satirists at *Private Eye*.

It was through Malcolm that I, hopefully, learned some of the heart, mechanics, and discipline required to write… a bit… and to study the corrosive machinations and magic tricks of power – from every angle.

HOW CLATTER IS THE WORLD

How clatter is the world
and mishmash and bashed in
and shrill with its blind throat songs
and strutting;
a peeling promenade in the desert
leading to no ocean,
and as wise as an oaf.

No longer tranquil with its own initial brilliance,
it became all this so much less than itself.
Gaudy and scant on a ragged red carpet
accepting venal awards,
adulation induced.
Its psalms vanished, its present canticles, coarse.
Adrift from the once sustaining memory
of its commissioning, its consecrated energy.
The blessing from the Throne.

It seems it has forgotten that everything in it is good
and soaring and curious and expansive, like
the opulent foxglove
the baffling tapestry moth
the fanfare of the lion's yawn.
All this now blanked out;
even the gemstone sound in its furnace,
its kiln and core.
How clatter is the world… and bereft, banished from
itself.

And yet, even now in its groaning, low months,
and while staring at its rundown wardrobe,
it thinks it remembers former talk of accession
and the promise of an imminent investiture.

9

EVEN WHEN WOUNDED...

A Simon and Garfunkel song "The Dangling Conversation" on the 1966 album *Parsley, Sage, Rosemary and Thyme* namechecks two leading American poets. With one I was already familiar, as I had studied him for O Level. The other was a new source to search out. The second is referred to a few times in this book.

I first heard the song around about 1968 on my friend John Mason's acoustically crisp stereo system in his grandparents' front room in Anfield. John's hi-tcch marvel of sound was a very impressive state-of-the-art beauty with "tweeters" and "woofers"... and "pingers" *(Pingers? Are you sure? Isn't that a clay animation penguin? Ed.)* So with a new poet to acquaint myself with, a bus ride into Liverpool city centre was called for. A meander around the holy grail bookshop of Philip, Son & Nephew Ltd in Whitechapel, opposite Brian Epstein's former headquarters, North End Music Stores, would ensure a successful search... and it did.

In the song, two heterosexual lovers are examining the emerging differences between them. Written mostly in the first-person plural, two eminent poets are cast as almost role-play contrasts in a bedsit drama accentuating the coming closing of the door on the relationship. Those counsel poets being Emily Dickinson for the female, and Robert Frost the male's companion.

Although Paul Simon has said, in hindsight, that it is one of his least favourite lyrics, there is an accurate angst and resonance in the one-act urban tragedy. The mirroring of the Frost and Dickinson personas serves a deft symbolism of disparity.

Frost was a Harvard-educated four-time Pulitzer Prize winner for poetry, who read (albeit with great difficulty) at President Kennedy's inauguration in 1961. On that weighty occasion, Frost had to abandon the recital of his bespoke poem, "Dedication". The combination of the brilliant sun's reflection off fresh snow and the poem, tapped out on a poor-quality typewriter, caused a heightened moment of uncomfortable tension for all. Ditching "Dedication", and ever the trouper, Frost went on to quote from memory "The Gift Outright", Kennedy's requested poem for the ceremony. In that moment, Hollywood happened. *The Washington Post* reported that the venerable poet "stole the hearts of the Inaugural crowd", which Kennedy had foreseen. The President had cannily booked a bardic plate-spinner and venerable scene-stealer.

It was the old lion poet's last hurrah on the world stage; the meticulous technician of the craft died two years later. In a strange apex-like ceremony in October 1963, a few weeks before Kennedy was murdered, the President officiated at a ground-breaking convocation for the future Robert Frost Library in Amherst, Massachusetts. On that day the President said that Frost encapsulated "the deepest source of our national strength". Amherst was the birthplace of the other poet referenced in Simon's song, Emily Dickinson.

In contrast, Dickinson, who died in 1886 of kidney disease, aged fifty-five, and who lived in privileged New England obscurity, saw very few of her poems published (some anonymously) in her lifetime. Her first collection, *Poems*, was published four years after her death by Roberts Brothers of Boston, who had also published Louisa May Alcott's *Little Women*. In death, Emily Dickinson achieved literary posterity through a groundbreaking yet commercially savvy publisher who championed women writers. In his speech honouring Robert Frost, President Kennedy said that the great artist "is a solitary figure", involved in "a lover's quarrel with the world". He could have been speaking about Emily Dickinson.

A poet is at the mercy and meanness of the muse seasons, and personal circumstances too. Bringing Robert Frost back to the podium, he saw the creation of a poem as "a momentary stay against confusion". For Dickinson, her expansive harvest against confusion took place during her twenties and thirties, when she wrote somewhere in the region of 1,100 poems.

When I go into schools to conduct poetry workshops, a question that often comes up is, "How many poems have you written?" Children are often fascinated by the "how manys" of life, the inventory of supposed achievements. I often finish my answer with. "… and your follow-up question could be… but how many are any good?"

With Emily Dickinson, even in the initially obscure poems, there is an exceptional journal of "goodness" and otherworld energy. "I cannot dance upon my Toes – No Man instructed me – But oftentimes, among my mind, A Glee possesseth me." Like her free-verse contemporary Walt Whitman, Dickinson's "unorthodox singing", notated by unconventional punctuation and yet on-the-nail metre, places her as a New-World original from that tumultuous, visionary era in American history.

Her letters also both fizz and stand still with a poet's restlessness, a not-belonging, answering-direct-questions "slant", such as in a reply to a prominent East-Coast writer who had asked for a picture of the poet "so that I might form some impression of my enigmatical correspondent". Dickinson responded, "I had no portrait, now, but am small, like the wren; and my hair is bold, like the chestnut bur; and my eyes, like the sherry in the glass, that the guest leaves. Would this do just as well?"

Allow me a small irreverence, but Emily *could* have come back with something along the lines of, "Sorry, the maid can't work this newfangled multiple-lens contraption. Just put me down as fragile and petite, with an emphatic barnet and wallflower peepers." Yet Emily's intriguing pen-picture of herself emphasized another innate characteristic of the poet (and most poets in my experience) – a perceived elusiveness, an innate desire never to be fully known, as that could remove their capacity to be invisible observers.

The enquiring pen pal was Thomas Wentworth Higginson, a Civil War combatant, high-born abolitionist, and supporter of women's rights. Higginson had taken to the pages of the *Atlantic Monthly* with a "calling all young poets" article. Unusually for the reticent Dickinson, within a month of the piece appearing, she submitted four poems; and so began an important correspondence between the spinster poet and the Unitarian minister and radical essayist, which lasted until the poet's death. Higginson visited the poet on two known occasions, and read Emily Brontë's "No Coward Soul Is Mine" at Dickinson's funeral.

Higginson was to become a pivotal figure in spreading the word-wonder ministry of Emily Dickinson. Seven years her senior, he advised the raw poet on the complexities of the craft, suggesting changes to her poems where he thought necessary. Dickinson accepted him as her "Preceptor", her instructor. In turn it would seem Higginson saw her as a work in progress, and hence did not embolden her to rush into print.

Following Emily's death, Higginson worked with Mabel Loomis Todd on editing *Poems*. Todd, a not-so-minor character in the Dickinson family story, had a long affair with Emily's married older brother, Austin. This was a shocking scandal in the respectable rural town. Mrs Todd visited the Dickinson family home on many occasions to, among other social provisions, sing for the household. She did exchange notes with Emily while there, yet they never met face to face. With Higginson, Todd set about selecting Emily's poems for publication, imposing titles (Emily often let the first line qualify as the title), meddling with the punctuation, and generally making everything "drawing-room orderly". Higginson, through his publishing contacts, steered the book through to publication.

What Emily would have thought about her verse being manicured for public consumption is, of course, not known. "The myth", as some in Amherst called her, attracted both fascination and disapproval, her reclusive domestic circumstances generating whispered asides.

The furthest she ever travelled was to Philadelphia, Washington, DC (her father Edward was a State Senator and lawyer), and Boston, where she stayed for some months in 1864 undergoing eye treatment. She lived a contained life out of which blazed a confessional of extraordinary lines and quatrains with vast variations of emotions, whimsy, and intellectual ponderings. She "felt a Funeral" in her brain. She "visited the Sea", where "The Mermaids in the Basement/Came out to look at me". She travelled in her head over battlefields and planets. She rowed through Eden, and "split the Lark", where she found "the Music".

And, all through her work, she hummed and hymned rhyming motets about the intangible metaphysical. "Behind Me – dips Eternity – Before Me – Immortality – Myself – The Term between – " with its trademark distinctive capitalization and dashes. The latter possibly suggested an Old Testament "Selah" – a pause, a "think on this" – although Dickinson didn't, as such, compose from a wholly fixed scriptural position.

True, she was brought up in a Whig, Calvinist household, with church-going mandatory. But such an independent spirit as Emily's was too free-form to be subservient to outward ritual. Her early grounding in the tenets of the Christian faith did give her an "accent" when writing poems that addressed faith, doubt, and the "Holy Spectres", but her alternative canticles soared beyond the jargon and patois of the pew and pulpit.

In an age when inflexible Christian dogma was on the ropes as the nuances of scientific discoveries and Darwinian concepts churned a deep furrow through the consecrated soil, by her late thirties Emily had stopped attending church altogether. In contemplative domestic seclusion, along with her beloved sister Lavinia and horticulturalist mother, after whom Emily was named, she cultivated a vivacious garden featuring roses, peonies, full bugle foxgloves, and zinnias.

And always there was her voracious reading, although she averted her eyes from the voluptuary Whitman because she heard that his work was "disgraceful". The family pile, the "Homestead", and the previous home, the "Evergreens", were self-improving, serious-thinking households, the bookshelves a feast of learning for Emily: from the fashionable Brontë sisters, Dickens, Burns, and Elizabeth Barrett Browning to the classics, *Pilgrim's Progress*, Shakespeare, and (despite her questioning of some of its contents) "the antique Volume – Written by faded Men", the King James Bible, remained a constant.

The frantically fertile writing period referred to earlier coincided with the American Civil War. This was to have a considerable effect on Emily's gossamer psyche. She will have seen photographs of the battlefields, "the oblique place" of war, considered the deaths of nearly sixty Amherst men, some of those Union soldiers known to her. Images of blood and suffering entered her poetry. "Sorrow seems to me more general than it did," she wrote to her cousin during the conflict.

I have learned much from studying Emily Dickinson's poetry down the years, not least that celebration and grieving can, and should, coexist in the same poem; for example, "Why – do they shut Me out of Heaven? Did I sing – too loud?" The very idea that exultant, child-like praise can lead to you being cast out and made to feel worthless is a moving, exceptional example of poetic antithesis – I would dare to say emotional and technical perfection in thirteen words, a herald of synchronicity.

I have used that coexistence concept as a starting point for "Even When Wounded...". I begin with the metaphor of the impaired fox (observed one afternoon from a window overlooking a large suburban garden) whose brief existence is blighted by restriction. But, unlike the fox, we can draw on resources from within to "unrestrict ourselves"; in so doing, even our limp may improve. To give the benediction to Robert Frost before the poem, "If poetry isn't understanding all, the whole world, then it isn't worth anything."

EVEN WHEN WOUNDED...

A raddled fox,
bleached rouge rear
limps over the soil bed.
One back leg has had it,
maybe an indifferent car, disease, or birth affliction
the cause of its hobble.
No crutches or mobility scooters for foxes.
Beneath the low skirt hem of a fir tree
the beast scrapes and scoops out the earth.
Though no longer fabled Reynard
or Fantastic Mr...
this task it does with arched back intent.

Sighting a provocative squirrel
in open lawn country, the dog untamed
stops its vigorous pawing, becoming transfixed.
An inert, telescopic sight, hair trigger ready.
Alas, not up to such sport now,
the reverie of the pounce,
it stares itself into disinterest as the squirrel skitters off.

Above, gliding parakeets are deep autumn raucous.
Leaf-loaded trees, cheered by a skipping wind,
throw russet confetti toward the fox
who has resumed its excavations.
How like the fox are we
that even when wounded we keep digging, telling
ourselves,
"This must be the way out. We should emerge
beyond the locked gate and the bitter, smouldering
compost,
fuming smoke of our past shocks."

Even when wounded
we are tunnelling in the hope of a right direction.

10

SOMEWHERE IN THE LIBRARY

The former American Poet Laureate Kay Ryan, taking a sleeves-rolled-up approach to writing poetry, said that for her, she has to "mechanically, intentionally, and wilfully begin". Add the trial and error "mix of clarity and mystery", as described by another past Laureate, Billy Collins, and you have the home-brew concoction of creating.

Poetry in practice could be likened to a chemistry experiment, the base element being the individual poet. To this is added a disparate array of reactive compounds – memory, observation, and especially books read with facts and information retained, stored away, and carried. Urban and rural images likewise, sights seen; from the eleventh floor of a tower block to a frozen field in Hampshire in January.

For example, studying the sorrowful oddness of a half-submerged piano in a canal. Why wheel it all the way along a towpath? Why was an upright made to walk a gravel plank? What solace tunes and arias remain in its drowning cherry-wood heart? "Cor blimey" music hall ditties? Cocktail-hour sentimental ballads? Who did such a thing to this dear instrument? An oddball literalist who'd had enough of Handel's Water Music? And so with such a spotting, the poetic process can start: what Paul Muldoon, 1994 winner of the T. S. Eliot Prize for poetry, describes as "allowing a poem from wherever it comes from… getting it into the world".

Back in the late 1950s, the Rawdon Library on Breck Road in Anfield was, for me, a principal agent in stockpiling the requisite components essential for my later poetic constructions. Interestingly (well, interesting to me and any organ scholars reading this), the library was adjacent to the late-1840s Grade II Holy Trinity Church, which could boast an early Henry Willis organ. Following his early successes in the provinces, Willis's thundering reputation as the foremost Victorian organ builder soared – so much so that by 1871 he had pulled out all the stops (apologies for that, couldn't resist) by designing and installing his then-latest great-piped beast in the Royal Albert Hall. In contrast, the Rawdon was a hushed world of enchantment and discovery where it was forbidden to even breathe loudly, let alone add a descant to "There Shall Be Showers of Blessings", faintly heard emanating from the pointy edifice next door.

Having learned to read at quite an early age, I signed up for my book voyage and was issued with three tickets, one for each chosen tome. Heading for the children's section, I soon discovered Billy Bunter, "Crikey, it's Quelch!", and Enid Blyton – "Excuse me conductor, but would this tram which indicates its destination is Dale Street take me to a 'smugglers' cove' instead? I do have lashings of ginger beer about my person. Well, a small bottle purchased from Kitto's at the top of our road, and some chocolate gold coins to pay for my fare."

Another enthralling intake was Sir Arthur Conan Doyle: a prototype Irvine Welsh without the graphic swearing, who introduced his young readers to the world of drug-taking as perpetrated by the troubled genius Sherlock Holmes. In *The Sign of Four*, first published in magazine form in early 1890, then as a novel, there is a clinical description of the detective pursuing his habit.

In retrospect, there is nothing shocking in Conan Doyle's depiction of a character submitting to his regular legal fix. Drugs that are now banned served as the cure-all de rigueur, especially among the educated classes of Victoria's empire. The new commercial drug, cocaine, and other psychoactive stimulants and soporifics like laudanum – liquid opium mixed with alcohol known as "the aspirin of the nineteenth century" – were available over the counter at registered pharmacists. In the ubiquitous manual *Mrs Beeton's Household Management*, opium is suggested as a standby essential alongside "Common Adhesive Plaster" and "a pair of Forceps".

As medical research began to reveal the harmful, and in many cases deranging, addictive effects of these opiates – culminating in preventative government legislation through the Dangerous Drugs Act of 1920 – so the physician Conan Doyle introduced "patient management" to his whacked-out sleuth. *The Adventure of the Missing Three-Quarter*, a Holmes and Watson short story that appeared in *The Strand* magazine in 1904, sees Dr John Watson weaning Holmes off "that drug mania" but realizing that that dastardly addiction was only just about on hold: "the fiend was not dead, but sleeping".

Meanwhile, on the bestseller list, a parlour full of poets and novelists, including Charles Dickens, Elizabeth Barrett Browning, and Bram Stoker, relied on available narcotics to alleviate ailments of the flesh and emotions, from gout to grief to migraine. While children's and popular literature of the nineteenth century could be said to have elements of "altered states" turning its pages, this was lost on the infant me. For I had entered the many-roomed mansion of big stories, dark places, and comic archetypes, marvelling at Billy Bunter's (also known as "The Fat Owl of the Remove") capacity to gorge on most of the tuck shop in one sitting. I was floating through this book palace high on imagination, my nearest brush with stimulants being a daily, unpleasant slurp of cod liver oil administered by my personal paediatric consultant – who moonlighted as my mother.

Later, in grammar school, came the syllabus-set poets, Robert Frost, Edwin Muir, and W. B. Yeats, a formidable forward line of modernism and ancient fable – a redoubtable trio whose words became my pretentious attempts at adolescent mysticism. With Yeats, in particular, "I went out to the hazel wood/ Because a fire was in my head". My poetic apprenticeship had begun.

Dickens, too, fanned the flames via the immense social tract of *Oliver Twist*, an inferno documentary in which Dickens' camera-close-up prose tracks London's dockside underclass, where hideous, terrifying brutes and trapped innocents coexist among base and violent shadows. And yet, thankfully for the reader, the foul and the manipulative do get their comeuppance, and hope, in part, prevails.

Keeping the film analogy and jump-cutting several decades, when I was the presenter of the weekly Radio 4 programme *Questions, Questions*, the company that made the programme, Whistledown Productions, had their office in Southwark. A short walk from Waterloo Station, the richly historic area permeated Dickens' early life, and, hence, some of his novels, for example *Little Dorrit* and *David Copperfield*. Debt, displacement, and dishonour are recurring themes in Dickens' sagas. He experienced the humiliation of all three when his father, John, as an insolvent debtor, was sent to Marshalsea Prison, off what is now Borough High Street, in 1824 when the young Dickens was twelve.

As Peter Ackroyd writes in his biography of Dickens, "Marshalsea never left him. The high wall with the spikes on top of it… the lounging shabby people." Images of confinement and degradation sound throughout the works of Dickens like a wail. For writers and poets, damaging childhood experiences surface in their adult work, in code or barely disguised third-person narrative. I sometimes used to go out and stare at the surviving wall of the Marshalsea in Angel Place, trace my fingers along the mildewed brick, and think, "Poor son, poor father."

Returning to my burgeoning interest in books, poets, and avoiding detention, it was in grammar school that I was first introduced to a book with a dazzling, far-out, spacey title: *The*

Lion, the Witch and the Wardrobe. I later learned that the writer, C. S. Lewis, far from being a strung-out Gabriel Rossetti figure, was in fact a beefy Ulsterman academic partial to beer, a pipe, and cigarettes. It was our long-suffering French teacher, Mr Wells, who, with all the sincerity of a fraught but persistent missionary, insisted on reading this wild and gripping epic, thankfully in English. I seem to remember it was on Friday afternoons during the clammy summer term. Some of my classmates – well, not so much mates, more very bright convicts who shared the same cell – weren't too taken with hearing about fawns carrying parcels and proceeded to doodle on each other. "Bomber" Wells, understandably, did explode from time to time, thus disrupting the plot, which I was following closely. I was traipsing through Narnia without snowshoes and it was intoxicating. And one important thing I was learning was don't trust the White Witch with your dinner money – you'll never see it again, or yourself, in any recognizable form.

The "message", if it is that, now emanating from these early learning experiences is that I am an evangelist for reading. Over the years, through my work as a children's poet, I have had, and continue to have, the privilege of going into many schools throughout the UK to lead poetry-writing workshops, give performances, and enthuse children to read. Reading is a transforming process, especially for children in frail domestic conditions, rooting them in the necessary educational principles of grammar, spelling, sentence construction, and the increasing of vocabulary. ("What do you mean, you don't know what a word means? Go and look it up.") It shouldn't need to be said, but for a child's future, literacy – the ability to read and write – is a vital requirement in the competitive job market.

Through the past few decades, I have observed successive legislative "negotiated reading" strategies implemented in schools, such as the Literacy Hour. I applaud this example of whatever it takes to get what at first may be disinterested noses buried in the tactile glory of a book. However, if you also suggest to our social media-sated, peer-pressured children that it's "really cool" to read, then the process can move on a chapter. I am of the generation that were made to read, no arguments or negotiation. Having said that, and having sat for many years in the small chair trenches of primary-colour classrooms, I am also aware that for children with physical or learning difficulties, or dyslexia, the approach has to be specialized and acutely sensitive toward the needs of the child.

But for the child not hindered by such developmental barriers, reading expands imagination, potential, and critical "wide thinking" while also giving children sustenance and respite before the grown-up world of dark knights and, sometimes, fraught nights sets in. I am keenly, possibly too keenly, aware that some of the children before me have experienced an early "besmirching". In these cases, reading can offer a temporary deliverance, an equipping, and a champion: an opportunity to advance into a momentary Eden before the Fall.

Two children's writers whose themes reflect the allegory of full combat are, as previously mentioned, C. S. Lewis and his fellow faculty member, and later friend, J. R. R. Tolkien. Tolkien's "blue remembered hills" of Eden, the literal Lickey Hills and Wyre Forest of his West Midlands boyhood, became the idyllic "Shire" in *The Lord of The Rings* before the wars raged. Likewise, the seven books of Lewis's *The Chronicles of Narnia* are steeped in the harrowing realities of warfare, ruin, and sacrifice before the long-way-off promise of restoration. Both Lewis and Tolkien dug into their respective trenches and went "over the top" during the First World War.

In April 1918, Lewis sustained shrapnel injuries to one side of his body at Mont-Bernanchon during the Battle of Arras. His left lung was pierced; "I concluded that this was death. I felt no fear and certainly no courage," he wrote. He also recorded, in Isaac Rosenberg-like imagery, "the horribly smashed men still moving like half-crushed beetles, the sitting or standing corpses". Tolkien's war record was equally frontline, and terrible. As a signals officer he fought in the Battle of the Somme in 1916 – "a welter of slaughter", as Winston Churchill called it. "Do you remember the Shire, Mr Frodo?… Do you remember the taste of strawberries?" Both Tolkien and Lewis subscribed to the belief that light overcomes darkness, the "true myth", but what hellish darkness had pervaded them as young men. "There are dead things, dead faces in the water" [Sam] said with horror…. "Yes, yes," said Gollum. "All dead, all rotten. Elves and Men and Orcs. The Dead Marshes."

When we read in Dickens of the incautious Wilkins Micawber genially grappling with the profit and loss of debt, or follow in Lewis's *The Last Battle* the devious, destructive behaviour of Shift the Ape, we are confronting momentous metaphors in the writers' life and experiences: their gyre, indwellings, and identification with the summits and whirlpools of the human range and spirit. Reading of such, which can make us feel less alone than we may feel, is to our benefit, our elevation, our deeper understanding, and our soul's nourishment.

The poem "Somewhere in the Library" "got into the world" because of one dedicated woman's mission. For many faithful years, Vivienne Thomas served as a community librarian in Gloucestershire and Monmouthshire. When she was invited to mark her retirement in October 2015, I wanted to give her a humble present – a symbol of admiration to say thank you to Vivienne, and her like, who keep our libraries open and as hospitable, imperative rooms of free resource. The library is sometimes a child's very first meeting with that spellbinding phrase "once upon a time", as it was for me in the Rawdon.

Vivienne had asked me down to Abergavenny for workshops in a couple of local schools, and to perform at an evening reception in her honour in the library in Baker Street where friends and colleagues gathered. It was a grand and moving occasion.

Vivienne didn't know I'd written the poem. It was such an honour to pay tribute to her in this small way. In the poem there are references (spot them) to themes and characters in earlier and contemporary children's literature – because "somewhere in the library…".

SOMEWHERE IN THE LIBRARY

Somewhere in the library
there are fierce, and friendly beasts.
Dragons, cowardly lions
enjoying midnight feasts.
Somewhere in the library
there are whirlpools and lagoons,
coves and crags and picnics
with pop and macaroons.

Somewhere in the library
there are smugglers' hidden caves,
and voyages and shipwrecks,
where adventures come in waves.
Somewhere in the library
there looms a Gruffalo,
and Twits and Gangsta Grannies
and a wardrobe full of snow…

… Where the White Witch turns the pages,
her icy fingers vexed,
as Voldemort is reading
what happens to him next.
Somewhere in the library

down a whizzing country road –
an amphibian with driving gloves…
the hapless Mr Toad.

There's a Stig, and Railway Children
all present and correct,
while underneath the floorboards
the Borrowers collect.
But somewhere in the library
there is someone very wise.
Her title is librarian
which is really a disguise…

… For she's a gatherer of magic,
and a confidante of elves,
whose legends she has catalogued
and filed on ship-shape shelves.
And she knows a thousand sagas,
and ten thousand thousand tales,
she's heard the yarns of hobbits,
and the ocean dreams of whales.

So, let me share her mystery,
one secret so sublime –
her special prayer that starts each day… goes…
"Once upon a time…"

11

THE MIND'S NOT WHAT IT WAS

Julian Barnes is a writer I have admired ever since I came across his 1980s novel *Flaubert's Parrot*, in part an erudite lampooning of literary criticism. In recent years, as a widower, he produced a most pastoral and penetrating book on "the state and the process of grief", *Levels of Life*. In the later part of the book he ruminates on his beloved wife, the literary agent Pat Kavanagh, who died in 2008. In the aftermath of her death, distressed by the losing of memories about her, a cruel second death, he lists his remaining remembrances – last clothes she bought, wine drunk, books read in those final times. In his mourning he is visited by the counsel of logic, and eschews suicide because, as her chronicler, if he does away with himself, he deduces so she will be annulled.

As a boy, he formulated the theory that the memory is a sort of left-luggage office to which we return later to pick up things we need. In a series of five radio essays under the heading *Changing My Mind* on Radio 3 in December 2016, Barnes (on reaching seventy) dissected what it was to remember and reflected on the mind and its relationship with time. Bringing his considerable intellectual heft to how time marks "our beginnings and our ends", he addressed all the multiples in between from, quoting Philip Larkin, the "forgotten boredom" of childhood to the shuffle and slippers of old age, and what our mind may, or may not, do with it all. Barnes was of the opinion that each time we roll up to the "left-luggage department of our brain", and take a memory out, a "degrading" takes place because time has, in effect, altered our memory of the memory.

I wrote the poem that kick-started this chapter – "The Mind's Not What it Was", with its simple, almost childlike rhyme structure – before I heard Julian Barnes's broadcasts. The poem is to do with mind and memory. Anybody of a certain age will recognize the clichés in the first part of the poem – the frustrating and annoying misplacing of everyday, functional objects, and the tricks that one then tries to play with the mind: the retracing of steps, the coaxing it to remember whether you did leave the oven on, as if the mind was a camouflaged saboteur, a mental fifth columnist with a mind of its own. "This will fix him – I'll move his credit card to his other jacket... Sound effect: echoey demented cackle."

The second part is a love poem where memory is a factual anchor: specific events that are unique to Carol and me; emotional "items" that are determined points of reference, heirlooms of our past. It is our left-luggage cognizance, which we can corroborate with each other, and is made more luminous by Carol, in some cases, "holding the history" of the moment – a reliable testimony that can remember what we ate, the weather, our respective moods at the time: the needle point within the broad tapestry of the memory.

Having set out to write a book attempting to explain how a poem may have come about, these accounts cannot be wholly linear. So it is with the writing of a "far back" poem; the lamp posts of memory are fixed but the detail of them and their sequence is, at times, nebulous, almost illusory. The creating of a poem is a blend of the sensate and intuitive, a mind high-wire act of the analytical with the necessary emotional balance to keep the poem in the air, in flight. A "finished" poem is both fixed and impermanent; a poem hasn't ever finished as such, but it has said what it has said, for now.

This may be unsatisfying gruel for the literalist expecting "exact representation without idealization"… but I would suggest that literalists make for blinkered and inadequate poets – that is, "This poem stops at the horizon because I cannot see beyond it." Unlike the owl, the literalist cannot revolve their head to see where they've come from (or maybe the bird is checking to see who left the door open because there's a nasty draught coming in from the back of the cage). The literalist also bangs his or her spoon if forced to bargain with the capriciousness of the topsy-turvy spectacular: for example, the male seahorse giving birth; the sequential hermaphroditism of certain fish… Surely, this is the devil's music?

Arguing against myself, and reverting to literalism, neither fish nor the devil plays music…? Well, I can't speak for the devil – but whales do sing, when alone or in pods. Science tells us, so far, that these aquatic arias are a courtship ritual, or for exploration purposes, and that these vocal displays are merely the harmonies of procreation and survival. However, I prefer to snorkel back to the "so far" proviso and adore the limitless beast as it breaches and bursts the ocean's film. I consider those songs as less so far but perhaps much more; the leviathan formed to play as the psalmist whale-watcher marvels in the Tanakh, the original source for the Christian Old Testament.

As the discerning reader will have gathered by now, I have never got on with literalists, nor they with me. I could give examples of my fanciful thoughts causing bedlam eruptions in alleged "creatives" over the years, but why waste page space? Rather, I call to the stand inside-out theologian Frederick Buechner, who, in the artist's defence, upholds and treasures such rampant nuisances as poet Gerard Manley Hopkins, "willing to appall and bless us with their tragic word". As the American poet and novelist James Dickey, whose book *Deliverance* was later turned into a lauded film, notes, poetry is "a fever, and tranquillity": a state of being that is both in sickness and in health, simultaneously.

So, when remembering such specifics as referenced in the poem that follows, such as Beacon Hill in Boston, Massachusetts (with its sloping cobblestone streets and elegant tall townhouses), I have only become aware in recent years that while the recall of being there holds both the factual and essence, primarily it is the essence that holds the facts for me in its cloud of knowing. The geographical locations mentioned in the poem do not subscribe to a child's neat journal account, a "my day at the zoo", a "then we did this and then we did that", but more impressionistic recall.

But having said that, I could give you some facts as to why we were in the historic area of old America, a well-to-do district that began to be settled over a hundred years before the War of Independence. We were there to take tea with the artist Conger Metcalf, an exquisitely dainty affair – although I couldn't tell you what dainties we had.

The drawing room in which we sat displayed the taste of an aesthetic man, a dandy dresser who twinkled with life and the best manners. We talked of art, the neo-Romantics of the 1930s who had influenced Conger, Blue and Rose-Period Picasso, and the light of Italy. It was a dazzle dream of an afternoon.

One irrefutable "fact" is that Conger sketched a pastoral portrait for Carol as we talked, and dated it "3/30/93". I'm gazing at the head-and-shoulders drawing of a young girl/woman as I write. And this is where roped-to-the-harbour-wall memory loosens its moorings; I would have said this took place in the autumn of 1993, not the early spring. Conger wrote to the right of the spontaneous vignette, "Please come back to Boston." He died in 1998, and alas we didn't get back to Boston to see him. Illness in our own house prevented that. Yet Conger lives on through his paintings in private collections and galleries throughout the United States, including the Museum of Fine Arts, Boston.

The poet Louis MacNeice, contemporary and friend of W. H. Auden, developed themes of cogent memory and impressionistic consciousness in *The Strings are False*, first published in 1965, shortly after his death (he died a few days shy of his fifty-sixth birthday). The book is the nearest MacNeice got to autobiography. It does not follow a timeline but rather allows a moment in time in the present to spark a return to adolescence and childhood.

As a poet, and later BBC radio producer, MacNeice carried in his verse the memory of the dislocating trauma of childhood. He was brought up in County Antrim in Northern Ireland, and his father became a bishop in the Church of Ireland. In his early infancy MacNeice's mother's mental illness saw her removed from the family home into a nursing institution in Dublin, where she died in December 1914 of tuberculosis.

Such devastation gave Louis MacNeice a sniper-like, acute focus of childhood: "My mother wore a yellow dress;/Gently, gently, gentleness" yet "When I was five the black dreams came;/Nothing after was quite the same". Those lines from his poem "Autobiography" were written in the late summer of 1940 in emotional exile in New England, when he was in his early thirties and far removed from the "childhood trees" of Carrickfergus.

Memory, when entering the attic of childhood loss, can clarify what was in a way "memorable" for the broken child in that place. (I was fifteen when my own father collapsed and died in front of me and the family.) In *The Strings are False*, MacNeice writes of memory going back and fading into myth. He ascends several flights of stairs of a house he lived in; under a sloping roof is a trunk that is locked. And there was a second house where his mother "kept being ill", but before that the wee boy, not yet separated from his darling mother, would get into her bed and listen to his cleric father in the downstairs study "communing with God". Because of what the "knowing" child supposed to be a "conspiracy" between the patriarch and "the Patriarch", the son became afraid of the father.

Such wounds in memories exist alongside, in MacNeice's case, the hawthorn hedges "flaming green in Spring" and "thick beef sandwiches with mustard"; the land of plenty with the "buxom, rosy" cook called Annie who had palpitations. In this awakening he, in delight, drew patterns in the soil under the laurels. The idyll before the dark lamp beside his bed… For this is what the poet is for: to trace memory for us and for themselves, and then colour it in with glowing hues and swirls of wonder… and descriptions of the carvings on the catafalque.

Returning to the Psalms (in this case number 137), there is an account of a collective memory lamentation of a people and their pining for their "land of begin again". The Jews in exile in a foreign land, "by the rivers of Babylon" after the destruction of their Temple, weep and remember "the highest joy" of Jerusalem. As to what unsaid else the Israelites were remembering preoccupies the interviewer in me, but, of course, it's a hypothetical question I am unable to ask. I can only imagine the drama that took place 2,500 plus years ago.

Louis MacNeice once wrote that "verse is a precision instrument", which it is. The tune that is played on the instrument, to quote another great Irish poet, Seamus Heaney, is ultimately "to be of service", and to paraphrase Heaney, especially in the memory of those things "blown over". The poem that follows has, in the manner of an apprentice, served its time.

THE MIND'S NOT WHAT IT WAS

Keys misplaced and names forgotten,
the mind's not what it was.
Letter lost and recall rotten,
the mind's not what it was.
Faulty spelling, password stumble,
the mind's not what it was
Words elusive, all a jumble,
the it what mind's not was.
Can't find car in multistorey,
the mind's not what it was
I call to mind enduring glory
the mind's both is and was…
You and me on Galilee, Manhattan in the fall.
You and me in silence at the Western Wall.
Watching otters roll then snooze in kelp off Monterey.
You in gold and me in blue on our wedding day…
Just found keys on window sill,
the mind's not what it was…
Hand in hand on Beacon Hill…
the mind's both is and was.

12

LESSON PLAN

When I first went to school, I had no say in the matter; I was not quite five and couldn't tie my own shoelaces. Nor could I converse in laundry-lingo Mandarin with Mr Kwok on Priory Road, who starched my father's detachable shirt collars. So, as the imminent September approached, there was no summer picnic in front of the coal shed with the towering parents where we could have workshopped and discussed reasonably the coming change in my work/life balance. Work? For what reason? Mater… pater… this is a wholly disruptive concept.

I arrived at Anfield Road County Primary circa 1957, give or take a bag of biscuits. As a first outing, it was a less than satisfactory pupil experience. I remember one of the earliest orders issued at the aforesaid holding facility being "to face the front". Not having legal representation to challenge the edict, I and my baffled comrades were all made to stare in the direction of Miss Sharp, or was it Mrs? And stare we did… sharpish.

However, had we but taken courage from *The Comet* comic role model Jet-Ace Logan, RAF space pilot and lateral thinker, and his pal Plumduff Charteris, we could have turned this inflexible command on its head – well, sat it on a stool and given it a Jammie Dodger. Just think what different perspectives could have been brought to the symposium if some of us had decided to face the back, or even sideways, or even started to defiantly whistle "Colonel Bogey" like those brave chaps in *The Bridge on the River Kwai*.

And there we have it, bemused reader. In the preceding paragraphs, we have shared an encounter with the ludicrous – by way of the speculative art of whimsy, slight goonery, and the sandpit jubilation of taking an idea and messing about with it. The poem at the culmination of this chapter, "Lesson Plan", is an exercise in the ludicrous, the ludicrous emanating from the everyday; the ludicrous, the adopting of a farcical stand, which magnifies the folly in which we sometimes find ourselves. Being "nonsensical" becomes, in those moments, an ad hoc manifesto, a solace and a small ascension toward a deeper truth. The camel going through the eye of a needle. The squishing of an enormous-bottomed elephant through a revolving door.

The poetic incongruity that will follow was caused by a hovering Ofsted inspector, bless him, during a day of poetry workshops I was conducting at a school in the Midlands. I had been tipped off beforehand that bureaucratic scrutiny loomed but it was a functional question on the day by the tasked official that allowed me to take off and be ludicrous, embellishing and exaggerating an imagined conversation between us. The question that I was asked was, in a way, alien to me although I understood the educational requirement of it. "Lesson Plan" is in this book as a result of requests I've had from teachers who've asked after my readings, "Where can I get hold of a copy of that poem?"

In this book, an exercise before I "hand in my dinner pail", I am showing you my scrapbook of artists who have, unbeknownst to them, tutored me through their dexterous wordplay and descriptive finesse. One of those, responsible for the aforementioned euphemism for dying – croaking, the final wheeze, and so on – is P. G. Wodehouse. Alongside him is another fellow ludicrous disciple, S. J. Perelman. It's not essential to be billed by one's initials to be a practitioner of the ridiculous, but it does add a cachet, which is former-age speak for branding. And who exactly is TK Maxx and why can't he spell Max?

Both writers, so different in upbringing and background but both sharing an early talkies apprenticeship on the Hollywood treadmill alongside writing for Broadway, have been, and continue to be for me, spirit lifters. To enter the Wodehouse mindset, a day spent in the company of his famous creations Jeeves and Wooster is to skip through a sunny meadow of contentment above which butterflies flutter, flap, and twang up and down attached to an angel's invisible strings of play.

The young gentleman lie-abed loafer Bertie Wooster has a taxing life. Some mornings, because of a mayhem-evening before spent in several guffawing establishments in what became known as W1, he occasionally feels too delicate to drink his breakfast. As the sparrows screech on a brow-banging spring morning, Bertie suggests that his brain-bulging manservant should partake breakfast on his behalf – this anointed attendant being the impeccable Jeeves, an ironed creature enriched with heightened, mystical intelligence and cunning. Jeeves could transform the top table of Mensa into a rabble of gap-toothed village idiots slurping straw soup.

For students of British comedy, where the nuances of class and deference can still form part of the sublime thrust and parry of respective comic foils, it could be suggested with some force that Jeeves and Wooster begat Richard Curtis and Ben Elton's Prince Regent and Blackadder. In both cases the mentally superior underling holds the keys to the kingdom of gratifying triumphs, not their dim dolt, supposed superior.

Wodehouse, public-school educated in top-hat, pecking-order Victorian England, was a lightning rod for amplified characters he had chummed up with in school, and later. Add to that fizzing, dotty plots where withering aunts, splenetic elders, and temperamental chefs bristle and roar just about this side of coherence, and the result is, as Evelyn Waugh – no acerbic comic slacker himself – expressed in a BBC broadcast in 1961, "a tonic from those suffering… from jadedness of outlook and dinginess of soul". And ever with Wodehouse, as with Perelman also, there is the standing-ovation, killer line.

In 1920, P. G. wrote to his adopted daughter, "Darling Snorkles" (Leonora Cazalet), about a dust-up he was having with Jerome Kern over lyrics for a Ziegfeld musical, *Sally*, soon to open in New York. Responding to a slight from Kern, P. G. lets rip. Well, more a measured gash. "The manly spirit of the Wodehouses… boiled in my veins – when you get back I'll show you the very veins it boiled in."

When Perelman, the only child of Russian-Jewish immigrants to America, loaded his fountain pen for the recounting of a sapping skirmish, in one case to T. S. Eliot, his words are less light touch, more visceral. Perelman had been dragged all around the capitals, from Madrid to the MGM Studio in Elstree to Paris, writing additional screenplay on the hoof for the 1956 film *Around the World in 80 Days*, for which he won an Oscar. But at what cost?

As Perelman informed Eliot in September 1955, he was at the frenzied behest of the producer, Mike Todd, described by the reticent, quietly spoken Perelman as "an indescribable megalomaniac… a combination of Quasimodo and P. T. Barnum… Even after almost a month's rest… when anyone addresses me unexpectedly, I still double over with the bends." Todd, briefly married to Elizabeth Taylor around that period, died in a plane crash in March 1958 in New Mexico, aboard his craft, *Lucky Liz*.

Over twenty years before, Perelman had served in the ranks of the Marx Brothers' gag infantry on the films *Monkey Business* and *Horse Feathers*, experiences that brought him close to stabbing his quill into someone, possibly Groucho. The Marx Brothers films of the 1930s are a cacophony of outrageous energy and stiletto one-liners. It would seem the real lives of the brothers mirrored the hoopla of their films.

Perelman had been hired by, mainly, Groucho, on the back of a reputation as a writer of sophisticated comic essays and fictions, notably *Dawn Ginsbergh's Revenge*, published in 1929. In 1931, Perelman and his co-writer, Will B. Johnstone, were summoned to The Roosevelt Hotel in New York to recite the script of *Monkey Business*. The two studious writers had taken an intense six weeks to complete their masterpiece.

At the appointed hour in the designated suite, they were the only ones there. As Perelman's biographer Dorothy Herrmann relates, around forty-five minutes later three Marx brothers, with their father, wives, and supported by "lawyers, dentists, accountants", firecrackered into the room. A snap of ill-trained dogs also snuffled in. Chico's wirehaired terrier set about Zeppo's furniture-chewing Afghan Hounds. Amidst the melee, Groucho entered with his wife, making twenty-seven people and five squabbling dogs in all. The diffident, sensitive Perelman drew the short straw and read the script, during which Harpo and others fell asleep. On completion Groucho offered his terse critique, "It stinks." Everyone left, leaving a devastated Perelman and Johnstone. The rewrite took them a further five months assisted by several other writers. In the end, nobody could remember who wrote what.

And so began a lifelong war of attrition between the painted-moustache comedian and the scholarly humourist with a real one. The two played out this *Sunshine Boys* long run until Groucho's death removed his rapid right-of-reply in 1977. Perelman followed a couple of years later. Their grudging respect and affection for each other was often submerged in searing acrimony – a not uncommon show-business affliction. But to take an example essay of Perelman's, "Farewell, My Lovely Appetizer", an intoxicating Raymond Chandler spoof, "I stared at her ears, liking the way they were joined to her head…. you knew they were there for keeps" has within it a consolation for the reader, a rejuvenating tincture against bitterness.

To research an artist's life with any degree of depth inevitably means meeting their rejections, personal sufferings, and unresolved messes. Both Perelman and Wodehouse resented their time in Hollywood, where the pay was good, the hours onerous, and as for their employers – the fickle, volatile studio chiefs – well, it seemed the ducking stool was too good for them.

In reading the considerable number of collected letters of both humourists, recurring themes occur, notably solvency, and the requirements for such: the travails of two highly literate, serious individuals confessing to privileged correspondents the woes of working in a shimmering asylum. Pelham Grenville and Sidney (Simeon) Joseph dashed off their off-the-record epistles to confidants, regaling them with teeth-gnashing examples of working for a competitive "general" market with only their wit and wits the means to supply the necessary "moolah" to support their expensive households. To add insult to the contract, there was no job satisfaction guarantee their scripts would make it to the screen as intended by the writers. Often they didn't.

That Wodehouse and Perelman were ravenous readers is confirmed through their letters. Both men started their careers writing for comic magazines in their native countries. Wodehouse, in time, established himself, during the First World War, with American readers via Jeeves and Wooster stories in the high-circulation *Saturday Evening Post*. Perelman progressed to the Elysian columns of *The New Yorker* under the patrician "let the writers be" editorship of William Shawn. Although Wodehouse was older by over twenty years, they were "twins differing", who knew that life is best combatted by shaking the jester's pig's bladder at it. The more burlesque and preposterous the better. Jokes… with purpose.

Returning to the lines and well-meant intentions of "Lesson Plan", the poem seems to have acted as a catalyst for teachers and support staff over the past few years, through my performances. Such good folk are, understandably, under the necessary scrutiny of the law and educational statutes. But without wishing to be contentious, if legislation is inflexible and doesn't have the generosity of merciful thinking and understanding when making its judgments about a school's deficiencies, then the "one size fits all" application can become a burden, and, in some cases, a disincentive to carry on in the inspiring and vital profession. I have visited a considerable number of schools that are beacons and bastions of "normality", a haven for the child, particularly in areas of social deprivation and family dysfunction.

Any report on the school's performance should reflect that more fully than it sometimes does. "Lesson Plan" does approach those problems subliminally but the poem's heart, its beating hope, addresses the development of the child, and the identification of each child's preferences, be they in the sciences, literature, drama, and so on – and for that preference to be encouraged, not at the expense of the child's "lesser interests" but acknowledged, and in alignment with.

LESSON PLAN

I could see it was a good school,
because the grass
growing out of the roof gutters
had been trimmed.
And the PE teacher who frisked me
for dangerous ideas
had cut his nails,
it was all very promising.

An educational official asked to see "my lesson plan" –
I said, "You're looking at it."
He said, "Pardon,"
I said, "That wasn't me,
it was that kid over there
with his jumper on back to front."

"So you haven't got a lesson plan?" he quizzed.
I said, "I will have when I start speaking.
It's all in my head.
If you like, you could prise that open
and ferret about looking for
non-existent target objectives
and tabulated forecasts
but, and I'm assuming here,
that motor cortex surgery
isn't your particular gifting…
and if you did go down that path
of opening up my temporal lobes

and then discovered you couldn't
get my neural plate to fit back in again,
it could distress the children,
and I don't think the caretaker would be too happy
with all that cerebrospinal fluid
splashing about his recently polished corridor.

"And besides, these neurological terms
are just words I like the sound of –
like 'subthalamic nucleus',
that could be a winning phrase in a limerick."

My adversarial keeper of the national curriculum tried
another tack.
He said, "You're being difficult."
I said, "I beg to differ. If I conducted the lesson in
Esperanto,
that's being difficult,
or had I brought a sea lion in to 'oinck' Tennyson's
'The Charge of the Light Brigade',
that's being difficult…
and would prove scholastically demanding.
To the metrically untrained ear
it would sound repetitious…
but possibly not to the sea lion
who'd be giving his all."

The interrogation persisted. He asked –
"How are you tracking the progress parameters of
identifying student outcomes?"
I said, "Does your mother know you use language like
that?"

But, anyway, let me put it like this,
the other week I asked a class
to describe their new school building as a simile,
and one lad said, "It was like a tropical sea... unique and
unexpected, like a policeman."
Another said, "It was like a new planet."
Another said, "It smelled of drains... and newly baked
chocolate biscuits..."

So, before I go into *this* class,
I'd say today's lesson plan
is yet to be transcribed,
but it exists now like prophecy
a divination
that the children will reveal in their own language...
if you let them...

13

… BE THE…

Although this chapter is a part-scrapbook of American cultural influences on my poetry and song lyrics, there *is* a related link to the poem at the docking of this chapter, "… Be the…". The impact of America on my creative processes has been further enhanced by many performance visits and stays there, as well as in Canada, over the decades.

The concluding poem, I like to think, has a sailor's rolling gait about it: a returning home, an end-of-voyage summing up, and "a sorting out and repacking" before a further sailing. A little mooring for now, and then the pellucid waves of the final ocean.

As I've written elsewhere in this book, the Liverpool of my generation was an ocean terminus, landing stage, and embarkation gangplank for the New World and the Old World, incorporating the evocative trading ports of the West African coast. The Liverpool waterfront and working docks were the source of livelihood for a multitude of street-dwelling and back-alley, marooned families. America, by way of transcendental contrast, became an imagined El Dorado of opportunity for mariners and travellers alike. To gaze on the broad ships recently arrived from New York at the Pier Head was less an I-spy exercise of noting the names of the luxury liners at anchor and more an invitation to stow away on the vessel's next trip. Go West, young man. Walk the diamond boulevards of Manhattan… and become more.

This untrammelled view and expectation of the promised land became tempered, rightly, in time, through going there, and reading informative books beforehand of those who had lived there and recorded the country's elations, becalmings, and desperation: notably, John Steinbeck's Dust Bowl plainsong *The Grapes of Wrath* and F. Scott Fitzgerald's unfinished groan against Hollywood, *The Last Tycoon*. For nowhere in this life is as good or equitably bountiful as we expect it to be. All fancied utopias are marred by deficiencies. The democracy of the elite that evolved following the American Revolution promised much, then became something else – what Martin Amis describes as "the remorselessly, the indefinitely gratified self" in his book of essays about American popular culture, *The Moronic Inferno*. Where there is no restraint or where there is a lack of empathy toward the undone, meekness ends up at a Skid Row soup kitchen, breathing the beatitudes of Jesus for solace and insight, the fortune of the excluded and the deprived.

Yet the intoxicating landscape of America, the arable largesse of its plains and groves, hinted at a responsible harvest for all with universal possibilities as envisioned in Woody Guthrie's "This Land is Your Land", though that settler's song, while idealistic, is incomplete in itself. Native Americans and their descendants say that the land wasn't ever "yours" – that it was always a borrowed space as opposed to an acquired treasure, a leased-reward to be shared. On my most recent trip to Canada, we were taken to an isolated Blackfoot Reservation in Alberta and learned something of the First Nation's encounters with European traders. The "Great Spirit" inheritance was removed from the original beneficiaries in pickpocket stages.

But what did the young offspring of seadogs know back in early-1960s Liverpool about colonization and the appropriation of land? Hollywood was our Wild West historian, and, as it turned out, an unreliable one. Meanwhile, merchant sailors were back on leave with exciting snaps of midtown towers higher than a giant's thigh, their kitbags swollen with talking-point ornaments, chewing gum, and plentiful nylons, and carrying hip and happening long-playing records to make a homecoming party jive alive. John Lennon's errant father, Alfred, had been a "merman", as had George Harrison's father, Harold. Those that were all at sea returned as stateside evangelists; the older ones retired to become alehouse raconteurs, booming and whispering their daydreams about the land of the free.

As early Merseybeat imbibed the sound, sentiments, and three-minute ecstatic love letters of Buddy Holly, Little Richard, and Chuck Berry, so their homeland – the root of their musical literacy – enticed. "Please, Mr Postman", where do I book my ticket to sail there? America, oh America… Meanwhile, I was listening to *Sing Something Simple* on the BBC Light Programme on a colourless Sunday evening in 1961. For me, this was the audio equivalent of being force-fed a never-ending Pontefract cake… those were long years, I can tell you. At home, even our optimistic Billie the budgie seemed to give up chattering when it was on, his grateful bell and mirror remaining unbashed. Or perhaps Billie was an intoxicated fan, soothed and made compliant by the close-harmony hallelujah to "Ramona", who heard "mission bells above" ringing out a song of love? Or then again, is it possible for a budgie to have tinnitus? Is that why my chirpy parakeet stopped the bell-butting business? A ringing in his feathered ears?

Anyway, as professional and accomplished as the Cliff Adams Singers – the programme's featured, and only, vocalists – were, they entertained our war-generation parents and grandparents on the wireless for forty-two years. For me, at that time, *Sing Something Simple* represented the opposite of what became Douglas Adams' meaning of life. Or to describe the transmission in the local patois, it was "dead antwacky" – that is, old-fashioned, cobwebbed with time; Great Aunt Mildred's chamber pot crooning out of a modern marvel, transistor radio.

Nowadays, I would probably settle down and appreciate the wordsmithery of former songwriters tunefully presented by *Sing Something Simple*'s tranquil arrangements. I may even put on a pair of zip-up slippers, complemented by a tweed bandana to complete the listening experience, and consider what Tom Waits would do to "Don't Sit Under the Apple Tree (With Anyone Else but Me)".

Before Liverpool's waterfront became salted with cranes, swinging cargo, and warehouses wafty with spices, the American author and poet Herman Melville wrote a postcard home of his time in Liverpool by way of his heave-ho novel, *Redburn*. In the early summer of 1839 he sailed from a Wall Street jetty on the merchant ship *St Lawrence*. This was the tenderfoot deckhand's first voyage, with the book being published ten years later. In an early example of a liverish Trip Advisor report, Melville, who later went whale hunting and got a parlour page-turner out of that too, let fly, "Of all the sea-ports in the world, Liverpool, perhaps, most abounds in all the variety of land-sharks, land-rats, and other vermin..." Yes, but look on the bright side, Herm. When the fog lifts, you can see Birkenhead.

By the time I made my first trip to America in 1986, I had a mulched mental chronicle of disparate references in the suitcase of the head. Carol had previously visited as a young woman, staying with her aunt in California. Her journey home then consisted of a three-day train journey across the continent, and then sailing from New York to Southampton on the *Queen Elizabeth*.

Courtesy of American Airlines to JFK, final landfall for us that glowing, audacious autumn was downtown Manhattan in SoHo, on the same street where the experimental theatre company The Wooster Group had their Performing Garage premises. This is a collective that reared the talents of actor Willem Dafoe, a founder member, and searing monologist Spalding Gray. At that time, the cast-iron buildings of SoHo housed galleries and avant-garde performance and dance venues. It was a buzzy artists' neighbourhood and playground. Alternative, counterculture, daring, thrilling. Basically, not a bit like Basingstoke.[3]

This introduction to America came about through an invitation by mime artist J. Geoffrey Stevenson to perform alongside him in what became a series of odd, funny, and anecdotal gigs. We did our silent and shouty stuff in a menagerie of venues, in and beyond the New York boroughs, and up into New England in the buffed-brass fall. There were shows in polite prep schools and small colleges; a retirement home where the audience were wheeled in, some politely asking their nurses to be wheeled out, soonest; and an uptown gay church that doubled as a radical Off-Off-Broadway theatre, in whose tiny dressing room a piece of advice was pinned up for the benefit of all performers – Vaudeville trouper George Burns advising, "Always take your wallet on stage." The great comic had obviously gone into a huddle with Herman Melville and compared their shocks and privations.

Our gracious, generous hosts were treasured friends of Geoffrey's – visual artist Caroline Stone and writer Rod Keating. From Caroline's welcoming loft in a former textile warehouse we wheeled out and about under the high-hope sun. On our non-performing days, we feasted on the architecture and museums of the city. And in my head, as if on a loop, the vaulting verse of e. e. cummings – the first lower-case, text-speak poet – sang, supplemented by the jazz-scat Beat poet Lawrence Ferlinghetti's 1958 metaphorical "circus of the soul", A *Coney Island of the*

---

[3] "Basingstoke? What does he mean?" Well, this is me chucking a comedy snowball. What Slough was to Betjeman, Basingstoke is to me: disjointed architectural functionality without Corbusier modernist flair, which leads to a quiet bleating in the soul for those who live there, I hypothesize wildly on behalf of the good citizens of this part of Hampshire.

Let's workshop this point a little further. A function of comedy/satire is to overstate by comparison. For example, Lower Manhattan and SoHo: a place of mythic-like inspirational buildings. Basingstoke? Unfortunately, not in my *I spy book of buildings* that make me swoon in ecstasy. But it's only an opinion: subjective, and a bit "muttery". I feel much the same way about fried onions, flip-flops, and fun runs.

Mind, a phrase attributed to Henry Miller in his 1936 book *Black Spring* (or *Into the Night Life*, according to Ferlinghetti).

Soon I would add my own small contributions in verse. Later came lyrics, self-initiated and supplied to singer-songwriter Martyn Joseph over a twenty-year period of collaboration. For those familiar with the works, songs like "Somewhere in America", "As Arizona Dreams", "Lonely Like America", "All in the Past", and "Archive" (those last two breathed into being by the humbling, outrageous Canadian geography, and touching on native displacement and Scottish and Irish expulsion history) would not have been written without the sensate experience of travelling and performing throughout America. The lyrics are comprised of condensed sketches of contrasts, and also conflict.

One of the problems of having read and listened more than a fair bit to other writers and recording artists, and been inspired by their lyrical geography and history lessons, is to perceive one's own limitations in that field. So, attempting to capture in three verses, a middle eight, and a chorus, the complexities of how America and Canada came to be with their different national sensibilities, and how those distinctive and separate landmasses appear now, is, and was, a difficult and elusive undertaking.

What follows here are some jottings of glimpsed dramas, the collected observations that became the permanent stories through poetry and songs: a concurrence of the myriad variations that inspired the writing of these memorials. Both the praising murals of nature *and* the tack of low-slung, Mall America...

... Idling at a stop sign in Florida, the sun a piercing, unrelenting spotlight, and watching a lean, young woman in scraped stilettoes and thin robe scurrying out of a door of a strip joint. She dashes along a stretch of dark purple wall and in through another door. She does not remain in the see-all light. Perhaps she assumes it will not accept her... An ambling armadillo in the same state on a suburban lawn.

Boarding a morning plane in Michigan with compressed

snow on the ground, to descend later that day over the furnace topography around Tucson in Arizona where all glowed rust. The gig that night in an art gallery… here in America; stallion-wild with cactus sculptures, and sepia wagon trains. Land of the free and displaced, with new songs nightly from the lounge of the cliché motel.

The last gig of a Canadian tour in Medicine Hat, the name translated from the Blackfoot language. The past unwilling to resettle elsewhere, because the past was the first one there. And before the performance on the very extremity of the town, I call Carol on my iPhone and ask her to listen to the slow wind of the immense Prairies. Whitman heard America singing "strong melodious songs". Tonight Canada is doing likewise as the earth counts the indentations of the missing buffalo. In the beasts' honour, the gig went well.

And so the poem "… Be the…" puts its passport back in the bureau, and plans its domestic days that are only temporary. I continue searching for the telling images of the seen and thought, and its associated symbols… "America, you've seen some changes/ Though you've been there all my years/As a child you so loved Lucy/ As a man you drank at Cheers…" ("As Arizona Dreams", lyrics – S. H.)

…And having written that, soon will be *the* big adventure. No documentation or visa needed. Safe and dangerous, a harbour and a hooley.

... BE THE...

Let these be the luminous years
the ludicrous, handstand years
the three-card trick
the tipsy sobriety years
the tickling bishops
and teaching pigeons to belch years
the elated, lamentation years
the consider the lilies years

These must be the forgiveness years
the admission years
the, as much as I've been wronged,
so have I wronged years

These should be the inward years
the hearing years
the radio properly tuned years
the stage mask removal years
the "behold the naked tyrant" years
the mocking the despotic
and that's including me years

Grant these be the wide years
the high years
the lavish and sedate years
the increments of radiance
and dying by such means years
the fixed point, not pinned down years

the pointless, with a point years
the how much I don't know years

So, let these be the praise years
the purging and the blithe years
the justice will prevail years
the howling with the harmed years
the solitude, less words years
the less and less and more years
the joke of empty tomb years
the reverent, don't care years
the knowing I'm beyond years
the being loved… that's it… years

14

THE AVENUE

The Avenue (in Liverpool's Anfield district), with its drowsy, two-strides-across, lawn-trimmed summers, evokes the second area of the city I lived in from about the age of thirteen. But it is the first home that emotes a specific smell and sound memory – that of the intoxicating scent of shoe polish and the high-note song of a cobbler's rotating wheel…

In the final years of his life, Ray Bradbury, who died in 2012 at the age of ninety-one, received the equivalent of a writer's honorary Oscar – a Pulitzer Arts citation, joining a pantheon of American artists similarly endowed that includes Thelonious Monk, Bob Dylan, and Hank Williams.

The accompanying 2007 tribute made mention of Ray Bradbury being "an unmatched author of science fiction and fantasy". Although the originator of such cultural commentary works as *The Martian Chronicles* and *Fahrenheit 451*, both published in the early 1950s, the writer distanced himself, at times, from such categorization. On the publication of *The Martian Chronicles*, Bradbury stated, "I don't write science fiction. Science fiction is a depiction of the real. Fantasy is a depiction of the unreal." And so the publisher's beckoning back-flap copy gave the bookshop browser some idea of what they, the publisher, thought Bradbury was: by all accounts, a sunny, optimistic man who couldn't afford to go to college so he went to the library instead, undergoing an adolescent educational transfusion through the epic myths of Jules Verne and Edgar Rice Burroughs.

However, it is another of Ray Bradbury's equally compelling books, *The Illustrated Man,* that has remained vividly in the mist of my memory, a present shape in the drizzle, even though I first read it nearly fifty years ago. Almost trance-like in feel, *The Illustrated Man* is a book of intense moods and roaming imagination. On first reading it had an immediate, hypnotic effect on me. Published in 1951 and made up of eighteen short stories, Bradbury employs a fascinating linking theme throughout its narrative. Considering when the book was written, technology having created, by then, the collective mechanism of two atom bombs that killed over a hundred thousand people at Hiroshima and Nagasaki in August 1945, *The Illustrated Man* has an almost prophetic-still warning about it.

Running through some of the stories is a mourning, Old Testament-like tone, which I would sum up as: where are we as holy beings in the midst of the unholiness we have, and are bringing about? The consequences of rampant technology and the effect on human beings as a result of unchecked and subjectively debated "advance" is the recurring disputation. The persistent question asked by the book is: is there, or will there be, an inevitable and self-fulfilling demise of humankind because of the consequences of "all this science"?

Within the book there are also moments of counterbalance to the frenzy and fury of invention. The possibility is presented that the creative imagination can also repair and elevate us. This is gloriously considered in one of the stories, *The Rocket.*

A number of the plots and action have a space, and distant-planet, scenario. For example, in *The Rocket*, a junkyard is the setting where the main character, Fiorello Bodoni, considers the night sky and imagines travelling beyond the moon to, even, Mars. This he achieves, with his children as passengers, by way of intensity of imagination and the zenith of fancy. Bodoni purchases a full-scale model of a rocket, straps his children in, and invites them to "feel" the journey, a simulation of the senses that becomes a real experience. As his children sleep, they become travellers.

But it is the method that Bradbury uses to draw the reader into the stories that makes it so extraordinary. In the Prologue, the "narrator" is hiking through the Wisconsin terrain when he encounters a man, William Philippus Phelps, whose body is a vivid manifestation of tattoos. The narrator is censured by Phelps not to stare at the depictions on his skin, for in so doing they will begin to "tell themselves", with some alarming outcomes. The narrator cannot help himself, and these tales, in effect riveting "films", play out.

It becomes evident that Phelps is psychologically damaged by his technicolour torso. He inhabits an inconsolable, afflicted present. Because of this, he is searching for the witch from the future who did this to him with her "magic needles" in order to kill her. At night the tattoos change and foretell the future; and, given time, the viewer's own. *The Illustrated Man* is unsettling, captivating, and weirdly contemplative, depending on which story is being portrayed. Unfortunately for those readers who prefer a satisfying conclusion, the book delivers a troubling, ambiguous ending. *The Illustrated Man* could be, perhaps, regarded as a precedent for what later came to be known as "magic realism".

Some of *The Illustrated Man*'s "lost chord" impressions might be detected in my poem at the end of this chapter, "The Avenue". While the subject matter is very much earth-bound, the poem is a distant star almost: a return to a past sky in which the illustration lives on, illuminated. A looking-back that remains in the now.

The poem is certainly geographically specific. Liverpool is cast as a brief, post-war, mid-1950s halcyon of making things presentable again, a tidying away of the previous engulfing, worldwide conflict: the period that roughly spans after Suez and before Vietnam, when Britain was going through "imperial downsizing", as perceptively described by comedian and history buff Al Murray. In "The Avenue", this low-hum transition is taking place in the far background. Meanwhile, in the foreground, a child's black-and-white impressions and observations are noting the determined "scurry and gathering" of grown-ups. These "case notes" blur into the adult–child's later awareness of collages of stories; in this case, of muted pastels, in which the observed are "not making a fuss". The poem is also a composite, ending with one woman's forbearance and service. We enter her story, listing her tasks, hearing the faint inventory of her heart, and hopefully we remember her, in her meagre, hallowed life – her glory unrecorded, until now.

"The Avenue" is a very diminished attempt at magic realism. By that I mean an illustration of a real world as experienced by someone, or others, unknown to us and whose circumstances, and reality, may be markedly different to ours. Magic realism invites the reader to experience compassion toward a character, or characters, in their different reality. The reason I've described the poem as "a diminished attempt at magic realism" is because in full production of magic realism, one of the most lauded examples being *One Hundred Years of Solitude* by Gabriel García Márquez, there are outside-of-time aspects taking the narrative on, but sometimes in an almost "jump cut" way. Time is often not a constant in magic realism, where ghosts, spirits, angels, miracles, and metaphorical symbolism are intensely ordinary, and expected. That feel of "other knowledge" is certainly so in *The Illustrated Man*.

The montage of "The Avenue" records small, everyday events that take place within a historical framework. But perhaps "The Avenue" is closer to a short impressionistic documentary than anything else: the memory as camera, much like the photographs taken by Harry Ainscough during Liverpool's architectural foment of the 1960s and 1970s, a book of "as it was" images that the brilliant and merciful playwright and, of late, exquisite painter Willy Russell introduced me to a few years ago. Or in the masterly spirit of the

2008 film–poem *Of Time and the City*, by Liverpool-born Terence Davies, in which the director recalls his "blue remembered hills" of swings padlocked at day's end and car-less streets, soundtracked by Sibelius, Mahler, and the Victor Sylvester Orchestra.

In those streets, artists of my and Terence Davies' generation were taking magic realist notes, studying angles, imagining a metaphor for a seagull, or watching the daily wanderings of the ubiquitous stray mongrel evident on numerous Liverpool bombsites. Perhaps it was always the same dog in a series of different shots, but not having the money for a bus fare he just moved around a bit – a canine who circulated. As Davies recognizes in his commentary to the film, "We leave the place we love, then spend a lifetime trying to regain it." In the final years of his life, when he lived in the Dakota building on Manhattan's Upper West Side, paparazzi shots show John Lennon wearing his Quarry Bank Grammar, old school tie. A garment for lament of what once was? John Lennon's "across the universe", New World surroundings a reminder of how far he had travelled in order to return, "trying to regain it"; Lennon's lyrics, especially in songs such as "Penny Lane", "Strawberry Fields Forever", and "In My Life" are vivid journal jottings of impressionistic retention. We are annals of symbols, outer and inner.

In the manner of *The Illustrated Man*, returning to my home before "The Avenue" we enter a brick-built work shed in the backyard of the rented ground-floor flat where we lived for the first thirteen years of my life. The one-man factory belonged to Mr Jarvis, owner of the whole property, who lived in the upstairs flat with his wife and family. He worked as a shoe repairer in one of the big stores in Liverpool city centre, but presumably undertook private jobs – hence the sole trader enterprise. I had not yet fully developed the journalistic skill of asking the key questions. Being six has its limitations.

Sometimes I would stand in the workshop doorway and inhale: a diminutive, shoe-polish junkie, high on Cherry Blossom

Black and Brown, absorbed by the small sparks emanating from the cobbler's wheel, which dazzled the dark air as steel tips were attached to brogues and smoothed off. Wearing a waistcoat and collarless shirt, Mr Jarvis would keep nails in his mouth alongside his cigarette. He was a leather-preserving artisan who never once got them confused by hammering a Woodbine into the base of a ladies' court shoe from Dolcis, with their cross-over straps – stylish footwear for the Works Dinner Dance at the Adelphi.

There is no denouement to this "illustrated man" tattoo. The essence and the theatre of shoes being fixed remains but it is the present that now resides. The last time I returned to that part of Anfield was when I was contributing to a Radio 4 feature on tourist Liverpool. Seeing me standing in the middle of the road talking into a microphone attracted a gaggle of local children wanting to contribute, but they couldn't work out why there wasn't a camera: spontaneous interviewees who one day may remember this, their "present", as I have in "The Avenue". One lad, the size of a sixpence, told me he didn't play with girls any more because they ended up bashing him… now that's what I call reportage. The house stood behind me watching, and nobody but me could smell its history.

In the intervening years since completing that radio report, I have learned that asylum seekers from the Middle East have come to stay in our former flat. The centuries-old ministry of Liverpool continues as a shelter for refugees, washed ashore through exile, famine, war, and displacement, shelters evolving into permanent structures that become settled neighbourhoods, for a season; a sustaining of the prevailing ethnic and cultural kaleidoscope.

"The Avenue" may give an impression of permanence but the last four lines confirm that it was brief. Yet to the child it felt like always and forever, and in a way it is. It is magic and real, and its illustrations have not faded. They have become archive as opposed to nostalgia (which I regard as a narcotic, a chemically altered longing for a past that presents itself as more idealized than it was). The past is a ghost, a spirit, a miracle. And maybe all of the above and what follows contains elements of what Liverpool-born author and poet Nicholas Murray characterizes in his book about the city, *So Spirited a Town*, as "the most ardent patriots are the absentee patriots". Make that, in my case, a patriotic, not-belonging, thinking-of-elsewhere patriot.

THE AVENUE

After the bombing…
… the war wounds of gaunt gable ends on show,
and then the trestle table, victory teas;
… came the hope.

The sprightly Saturdays
jaunty with shopping –
turnip, carrots, and small lamb chops.

The ironmongers,
a counter cordoned with
clothes pegs, soap flakes and paraffin, carnation pink.
If the place ever caught fire,
it would be suds, charred, wishbone-shaped wood and
cinders.

Further up the Avenue
the regular mouse, black rosary eyes,
in the chip shop window
content in its fat firmament.

The shopping bag scurry and gathering
and then tending the house
that seemed always in shade.

You, inside, polishing someone else's sideboard.
The sawdust on the butcher's floor,
that too, like you,
not here nor there… anymore.

15

OCCUPY

Things to do today. Pick up dry cleaning. Have hair cut. Remember to spell "mnemonics" correctly. And you thought your life was humdrum. Then this evening, look up at the night sky and start writing an allegorical poem about the Apocalypse. Probably not with bluebirds skittishly circling one's head in the last line, given the ruinous subject matter.

The resulting poem, "Occupy", stares back at us at the end of this chapter. Make of it what you will. However, I recognize two specific influences that brought about this poetic planetary excursion. There are, in fact, a few more components idling on the subs' bench, including intimations from science fiction invasion literature, notably *The War of the Worlds* by H. G. Wells. Even now, given its late-Victorian, rolling-eyes sensibilities regarding imagined other-world beasties, the book is still a whole-box-of-liquorice-allsorts page-turner.

But to return to the two specific influences in "Occupy". In March 2017, Sir Richard Branson announced his latest high-flying development, Virgin Orbit. Part of his dream portfolio is to bring commercial space travel to, if not our generation, then possibly our children's. In the words of the "let's make the impossible possible", new-wave businessman, the venture is intended "to open access to space to change the world for good".

"Occupy" blasts off into a deliberately overstated tangent: a counterbalance to the rush to inhabit that which we do not fully comprehend, nor have we scrupulously assessed or, perhaps, even respected. Learned environmentalists can provide examples of the shameful damage done to this planet, where reasoned stewardship has ended up occupied and contained by ignorance and the desire for profit. Why should space evade a similar devouring?

For ten years I was the presenter of the fact-finding programme *Questions, Questions* on BBC Radio 4. One of the numerous features we covered was on how many satellites are orbiting the earth. With the expert help of an astronomer from University College London, we peered up the galactic stairs. The professor taught me to satellite-spot those blinkingly visible to the naked eye. The final census (and this was a few years ago) was around about 3,000 and rising. According to the United Nations Office for Outer Space Affairs, the 2016 figure was 4,256, of which only about a third were operational. Given that some of these craft have short-period lifespans, and then add to those the obsolete space junk that's accumulated over the sixty years before, it is reasonable to conclude that James T. Kirk's "the final frontier" is a technological fly-tip.

"Occupy" is a beseeching note in the margins, a pining-note pinned to the village noticeboard regarding unheeding the consequences of rampant expansionism: an Ecclesiastes-like, minor paraphrase that cautions that wherever humankind travels, the best and worst of steeds are hitched to the wagons.

The second, and probably the dominant, influence in the poem comes by way of a nineteenth-century poet with erratic health and nature – an Oxford double-first intellect, who could converse in Latin and wrote some momentous evocative "looking up" meditational poetry.

Following his arrival in 1870 at the seminary, part of St Mary's Hall, Stonyhurst, near Clitheroe in Lancashire, the Jesuit priest and poet Gerard Manley Hopkins recorded a remarkable sighting.

Back in the days when pitch-black nights were part of the rural, seasonal rhythm, Hopkins was awed by a luminous sky. "First saw the Northern Lights.… This busy working of nature… was like a new witness to God and filled me with delightful fear."

It could be said that the poetry of Hopkins was at its exalted finest when he pondered the natural theatre of the ambrosial. Whether it was the colour-saturated spread of a miraculous sky, or the differing shapes and density of hailstones, Hopkins not so much wrote poems in praise of creation but drew it in exuberant words and quirky, racing rhythms: descriptions that acted as messengers telling of the strange majesty of planets and songbirds and divine imagination. In contrast to the fleshly and subservient restrictions of his religious calling (which demanded celibacy, and submission to his elders), the muse-language of Hopkins roamed sensuous and expansive: sonnets of luxury and abandon, free-verse hope and wonder; an open-door confessional asserting the "immortal diamond" shape of Christ in the firmament.

After St Mary's Hall, Hopkins' further studies took him, in 1874, on to St Beuno's College, near St Asaph in North Wales, where, according to his biographer Professor Robert Bernard Martin, Hopkins wrote some of his "undisputed masterpieces", such as "As Kingfishers Catch Fire", "The Windhover", and "Pied Beauty". Yet as Professor Martin informs in his meticulous study *Gerard Manley Hopkins: A Very Private Life* (published in 1992), Hopkins (who died in 1889 in Dublin) was in fellowship throughout his forty-four years with those besetting companions of poets – melancholy *and* not fitting in anywhere much. This, in turn, when internal balance deserted him, led to alarming depression and a gothic preoccupation with death.

But when Hopkins was above himself, unperturbed and un-haunted by the lowest taunts of his moods, he reached Whitman-like levels of balloon-blowing joy. In correspondence with his friend from University of Oxford days, and later Poet Laureate, Robert Bridges, Hopkins revealed that he had, indeed, read the

American modernist. Bridges thought he identified Whitman's influence in Hopkins' poem "The Leaden Echo and the Golden Echo"; Hopkins explained, perhaps a tad defensively, that this was more for rhythmic research purposes.

Reading the poem today with a twenty-first-century mindset, its rapid tumble of images would seem to fit very well in the rat-a-tat delivery repertoire of today's urban spoken-word artists, and hence a reminder that there is nothing new under the sun. All poets, consciously or unconsciously, are saying nothing new but, rather, what is new to them and to their audience, and, as such, is new. As ever with poetry, the wizardry is in the telling, the entrancing of words.

I can't remember when I first came across Hopkins' poetry; it was probably in one of the many anthologies I devoured sometime after I left school. Certainly his poem "God's Grandeur" piqued my attention: a sonnet of humble adoration and keen content exemplified by the line "There lives the dearest freshness deep down things". Immense themes dance within the technical confines of this difficult-to-master poetic form. I quickly realized I had been introduced to a poet of many layers and set about finding out more. While at Oxford, Hopkins remained, externally, a High Church Anglican until 1866 when he was received into the Roman Catholic Church by his recruiting mentor, John Henry Newman, who had made the same journey twenty-one years earlier. For Hopkins, this "true" process conversion was generated by the usual, high-minded suspects – which Church could claim the pre-eminence and purity of doctrine and authority of Scripture? Although in recent times the ecumenical movement has gone some way to softening the divisions between Catholic and Protestant beliefs, it was the Liverpool connection in Hopkins' ministry that furthered my interest in the piety of the poet's life.

In the final few days of 1879, Gerard Manley Hopkins arrived as a select preacher (junior curate) to a Jesuit showpiece church,

St Francis Xavier (SFX, as it's known to locals today), in what was then the largest Catholic parish in Liverpool and besieged by Victorian levels of poverty. The surrounding area was to become the poet's mission field. Alas, it was not to be a rewarding calling for one of God's acutely sensitive servants.

The church, in Salisbury Street, had been opened in December in 1848 in a little-populated, but rising, well-to-do district. Although only a few miles from the expanding waterfront, it was then at the city limits. Within walking distance was the also recently opened Liverpool Collegiate Institution for boys, a solidly Protestant, educationally liberal establishment, where in 1843 the later Prime Minister William Gladstone gave the inauguration address. (The Collegiate became my grammar school during the 1960s.) With handsome terraces and villas being constructed, the locality was growing.

As a Jesuit and, hence, under the unwavering discipline of the Society of Jesus, a Catholic order founded by St Ignatius of Loyola in 1540, Hopkins knew that he was likely to be sent, without question, to wherever his elders decreed. By the time Hopkins had taken up his clerical apprentice post, the neighbourhood teemed with thousands of Irish immigrants, who, having fled famine in their homeland from the late 1840s onward, found themselves in desperate circumstances. Large families crammed into abysmal slums, relying on the church for on-the-parish support and brittle spiritual sustenance. Their humanity and worth was further eroded by the strident anti-Catholicism of the Orange Order, with their provocative summer marches past St Francis Xavier, the air graffitied with flute-fuelled tunes denouncing the pope.

Within the sectarian maelstrom of Everton, Hopkins' exhausting duties consisted of visiting the sick and dying – a task, rather than a beholden and accepted calling, to which the squeamish and rigid Hopkins was not temperamentally suited. Years later he wrote, "... to what filthy places have I not myself carried the Lord of Glory! and worse than filthy places, dens of shame." The suffering and privations of others accentuated Hopkins' own emotional afflictions and inner commotion, as is evident in some of his tormented letters.

Alongside his fellow priests, Hopkins was also called upon to preach his learned, esoteric sermons to pews packed with the respectable and the ravaged. Hopkins' discourses were not received with favour by either his socially diverse flock or his clerical instructors. On the poetic front, during his eighteen-month tenure at SFX, Liverpool proved to be a creatively barren outpost. The one poem that stands out from this dry period is "Felix Randal", dedicated to a thirty-one-year-old farrier who died of pulmonary consumption in April 1880.

Viewing Hopkins now from the materialistic expectations and excesses of the twenty-first century taxes the modernist's rationale. In his increasingly reclusive latter years, the poet's sincere dedication to abstemiousness and abnegation could be regarded as unhealthy and freakish. Yet I would suggest that this is to misunderstand the earnest strivings of his devout heart. Hopkins was a peculiar amalgam of external forces and inner drive. Life for him was both the sternest of sacred examinations and conversely a pilgrimage toward transcendence in which the ebullient, "dazzling whitewash" of God persisted "wherever an elm arches". His abstract, extravagant verse contradicts his austere demeanour. Hopkins was a poet not altogether of this world who directed me to look up, and to scan and explore, with the inner eye.

OCCUPY

We have not, as yet,
begun to quarry the moon,
opening it up to pilfer its mysteries,
the source of its beams and
songs of dark side beasts…
but it will come.

And when the excavations commence
a picket line of angels
indeterminate in temperament,
having heard the sound of gouging excavation,
will arrive
void of celestial etiquette and howling with hooch.
That illicit still they'd kept concealed
in a crater on Almathea
had not evaded God, though.
His broad eye sees all, yet such vision has wearied
Him… Her… Them… who knows?

Inevitably, there will be a stand-off.
The angels will subsequently argue over tactics
and divide into factions.

In time, missile bases will be constructed.
The Seraphim, sensing defeat, will disperse and flee,
the remaining Cherubim will be rounded up.
Opportunistic Malachim,
ever the pragmatists,

will accommodate the new regime
and as foretold, the moon will be owned,
it having suffered under flags before.

And we, as colonizers, will be industrious
with infrastructures, timetables, and sentry boxes,
instigating the ritual of gin slings
and backgammon evenings.
All the while unaware of
the gathering hooves of Mars.

16

ANY SECONDS...?

I first encountered the morality tale that is *Macbeth* in grammar school. It was the set text for O Level, and it has remained with me ever since – particularly the spectacle of the witches' brew of premonitions contrasting with Macbeth's haughty but spurious belief in his invincibility. The play remains intensely contemporary. The inspirational recipe for this chapter's poem takes its lead from the following "specials board"… "Eye of newt, and toe of frog, Wool of bat, and tongue of dog, Adder's fork, and blind-worm's sting, Lizard's leg, and owlet's wing", the chanted offering from the witches around their cauldron.

As al fresco barbecues go, let's file their plat du jour under "daring". I've had worse, as many touring musicians who relied on early-hours-of-the-morning motorway repast during the 1970s would testify. "Excuse me… would that congealed morass approximate the kitchen's lacklustre attempt at shepherd's pie? If so, I'll have a plate of fresh air, please."

My poem "Any Seconds…?" is a satire, a comic rhyme, doffing its culinary cap at Shakespeare's crones. "Any Seconds…?" transports the archetype, conical-hat embodiments of foul deeds to the present setting of "comfort and artifice television" and lets them loose. An imagining of three sisters of sorcery cackling their way through the *Great British Bake Off* tent, slipping hemlock and goat's bile into a sumptuous gloop of sherry trifle? How the ratings would plummet, or perhaps not. There is a sizable audience now for bad-taste television.

The influence of Noel Coward also contributes to the poem. His arch and witty lyrics are, and have been, a joy to examine and read. Some of his songs read like poems, rhythmically perfect with "light music" social observation. His early-1950s austerity sing-a-long, "There are Bad Times Just Around the Corner", is just one such sparkling, skippy example. More of that dynamite lyricist and playwright later...

But come with me now... to Act 4 Scene 1 of Shakespeare's tragedy, where the witches are throwing together their startling signature dish for Macbeth in a brooding, bubbling scene of high drama. As the ghastly concoction simmers away, the increasingly villainous king seeks further secret knowledge from the "midnight hags".

Macbeth's fate is foretold by cryptic words and apparitions, but the deluded king "hears" their prophecy on an incomplete, literal level, missing their catastrophic, veiled nuances. The gruesome and horrifying ingredients they toss into their cast-iron tub, specific to Shakespeare's time, serve as symbols for the darkness of Macbeth's brutally ambitious heart. Some of those symbolic descriptions rightly jar our sensibilities today, especially the ethnic references. Without going further into the entangled plot, Mr and Mrs McB are recipients of their just desserts (still the food analogies keep being served up). As the degenerate *House of Cards* duo assassinate their rivals, so, in turn, mayhem and downfall is their eventual inheritance. Macbeth is slain by Macduff, while Lady Macbeth's assumed demise takes place off-stage – as explained by Macduff, "by self and violent hands. Took off her life."

What Shakespeare shows each generation is how the political crises of their day are rooted in his dramas. The personality deterioration of King Lear and the machinations of Richard III repeat themselves. Deadly daggers or swords may not be thrust through the curtains of our courts of power, but intrigues and events supported by reason's savage words have seen off prime ministers and presidents in the democratic West in our own "threescore and ten". In his sombre and searing book on religious violence, *Not in God's Name,* former Chief Rabbi Jonathan Sacks regards the Hebrew Bible as "a sustained critique of politics... [and] the corruption of rulers". Shakespeare's caustic, purging dramas do likewise.

In the years since first hearing the witches' ominous and malignant press release, I have become familiar with the majority of Shakespeare's works and sublime sonnets. But in order to comprehend Shakespeare in his time, I have found it a helpful exercise to study what known writings and contemporary events influenced the Bard, taking in the ongoing, competing theories regarding the sole authorship of some of his plays.

For instance, in 2012 leading University of Oxford academics, including Professor Laurie Maguire and Dr Emma Smith, textually deduced that *Timon of Athens* and *All's Well That Ends Well* could have been written in collaboration with a contemporary of Shakespeare, Thomas Middleton. Middleton certainly had his uncomfortable moments when his short-lived 1624 smash hit, *A Game at Chess*, an early spot of Jacobean agitprop, ran for nine days before packed houses at the Globe. This was not good news despite the "tour de force" notices. The play quickly ran into censorship problems following some high dudgeon from the Spanish court, who sensed anti-Catholic sentiment. King James I ordered the play (a representation of how the State governs) be closed down.

And then there are the "this one will run and run" theories about Edward de Vere. This 17th Earl of Oxford was an adolescent graduate from Cambridge, high-born qualified, a much-travelled cove, an Italian speaker, and hence a trim-bearded cinch to knock out *Julius Caesar* and *Romeo and Juliet*, if indeed he did. I refer you to *The Man Who Invented Shakespeare*, Kurt Kreiler's frighteningly sized tome, for further reading. An urn of strong tea and several bolstering packets of fig rolls should get you halfway through the epic.

Other scholars have deduced that "Shakespeare" either singularly or collectively "borrowed" ideas from other cultures – *Hamlet* from a pre-existing Norse tale, perhaps. And pity the original eleventh-century Scottish king Macbeth, grieving in his very old grave, his reasonable reputation traduced by Shakespeare's rough redrafting and recasting as an enforcer, "because I'm worth it", royal apogee.

One essential element that *is* required in decoding key points in the plots is the use of biblical allusions in the dialogue. Just for starters, *Othello* contains more than fifty. Dr Naseeb Shaheen, former professor of English Literature at the University of Memphis, was a specialist in this field and published an exhaustive study, *Biblical References in Shakespeare's Plays*. With impressive scholarship, Dr Shaheen concluded that Shakespeare's familiarity with the Geneva translation of the Bible, published in England in 1576, in addition to other English versions then in accessible use in Anglican churches, provided the playwright with a rich source of device and character interpretation.

Along with the unsurpassed poetic flair of the plays – for example, in *Henry V*, the soon-to-be defeated Dauphin at Agincourt speaks to the soul of every tongue-tied horse rider, "When I bestride him, I soar, I am a hawk: he trots the air; the earth sings when he touches it…" – Shakespeare teems with gladdening greatness and lasting relevance in line upon line.

So exits Shakespeare, in this case not pursued by a bear, and on comes Noel Coward for this chapter's second act. The latter artist is certainly familiar with the former; and the former, as a workaday actor–playwright, would perhaps recognize the latter's self-taught-at-the-coal-face approach to the interpretative art. As Coward recalled: "It's no use… taking courses in acting. Better play to a bad matinee in Hull – it will teach you much more than a year of careful instruction. Come to think of it, I never did play to a good matinee in Hull."

Going through the biographies and diaries of Noel Coward is an important insight into the creative industry and exacting discipline of his working practices (and his kindly and practical support of fellow show folk going through career and psychological doldrums).

Coward's biographer Sheridan Morley sees the ghost of Shakespeare permeating key scenes in two of Coward's more lasting plays, *Private Lives* and *The Vortex* (the latter being Coward's grand arrival in London theatreland in 1924, with its scandalous drug addiction theme). To crudely contextualize (and I'm glad Sir Noel is not around to read this), *The Vortex* is shades of *Trainspotting* but among Jazz Age up-and-outs without the effing and blinding and appalling lavatory. One of the explicit Shakespearian connections Sheridan Morley detects is the impact and neuroses of Hamlet in the character Nicky Lancaster, especially in the audacious bedroom scene in *The Vortex*, a part Coward wrote for himself.

Six years later, Coward explored narcissism and moneyed indulgence further in *Private Lives*. Having once been married to each other, Amanda Prynne and Elyot Chase are on honeymoon in the same hotel in fashionable Deauville on the Normandy coast with different, rather dull spouses. After the shock of meeting up again, Amanda and Elyot begin to spar and regret with equal intensity within silk hand-grenade conversations. While the dialogue may use a lexicon that references and reflects their limbo, materialistic lives ("Let's be superficial," demands Elyot), *Private Lives* is a contemporary tragedy, fathoms deep, and with a comic twin-balcony scene: a subversive suggestion of what could have become of Romeo and Juliet had they not made a terminal muddle of all that potion/poison/dagger business.

For me Coward's popularist piece is not so much the theatre of cynicism but of realism. Amanda and Elyot's plight is a search for meaning. The validation of the self is their quest, and theatre is a participatory art; ours too. Amanda and Elyot's exchanges are pithy, trenchant tweets disguising internal, unarticulated soliloquys.

Coward learned from Shakespeare, who in his time was tutored by prevalent great texts. Both playwrights continue to speak to us in spotlit-concentrated musings on the eventual impotence of power, the waning of slight attractions, and the craving for purpose and place.

"Conversion" theatre stays in the memory and alters the perspective. Carol and I saw Simon Cadell and Joanna Lumley in the lead roles of Elyot and Amanda, back in 1981 at the Richmond Theatre. As actors they mesmerized, and the dialogue and the play's concepts, ditto. Coward's public persona of cigarette-holder posturing and elegant insouciance masked a deeply serious artist. I first came to his work through his various revue and operetta songs regularly aired on the BBC Light Programme, performed by Coward with his unique "the teeth and the lips and the tip of the tongue" diction and musicality. In songs such as "A Room With a View" and the society lampoon "I Went to a Marvellous Party", not one word is superfluous. And then there are Coward's screenplays for two of British cinema's venerable productions, *In Which We Serve* and *Brief Encounter*.

The late Dario Fo, Italian dramatist and winner of the 1997 Nobel Prize for Literature, said, "A theatre, a literature, an artistic expression that does not speak for its own time has no relevance." It is that continuity of relevance that Shakespeare and Coward keep giving and it translates to our own jangled times.

Dario Fo also saw satire as containing an element of the grotesque, a fright mask to make us recoil and reconsider that which may have seduced us. I make no such claims for "Any Seconds…?" but when I began to identify the poem's creative additives, I was surprised how early influences endure… and only having played squash once in my life, Noel Coward's counsel reminds me as to the debatable merits of all that thwacking exertion – "That's not exercise, it's flagellation."

ANY SECONDS...?

Double, double toil and trouble
How's my make-up? 'Scuse my stubble,
and my weird verruca lips
bleeding in the moon's eclipse.
Good job that we shoot at night
on blasted heath in shadow light.

Double, double toil and trouble
oregano, builder's rubble,
spade of landfill – Hades hot
squirrel snot in lead-lined pot.
Envenomation of black mamba,
chives and traffic warden's camera.
Car alarm and song of crow,
Yorkshire terrier's bright pink bow.

Mercury and zombie's spleen,
lavender and mildew green.
Lemon curd, our Aunt Elsie,
everyone off *Made in Chelsea*.
Glace cherries, fertilizer,
dash of Tizer, moisturizer.
Tarot cards and finger root
but no need for the eye of newt.

Tamarind and vampire's fang,
rough puff pastry, pink meringue.
Tarantula, vanilla paste –
tarmacadam for the baste.

Jasmine, basil, trail of slug
whisked beforehand in a mug.
Zenith of our baking skill –
season with a sprig of dill.
Drizzle with some gargoyle's breath.
Our next appearance – *Masterchef*.

17

EVERYTHING IN HEAVEN
COMES APART

Everything in Heaven Comes Apart" was written in response to a personally wounding series of events, which I found difficult to understand at the time and difficult to "settle". In their aftermath the words poured out one summer afternoon, with adroit input from Carol (making it a poem, and latterly a song, that we co-wrote together), when we were staying with friends in the Sussex countryside. The poem became an exercise in self-medication, an attempt at trying to make sense of why we do hurtful things to each other (the arts is a notable "slaughterhouse"). I very much include myself on this charge sheet. In "Everything…" the vast and the ordinary, like a jerky home movie with its seemingly unrelated images, all take their place in becoming parts of the whole. The "Heaven" metaphor is, I suppose, the sorting-out box, the light-filled, metaphorical cosmic attic where perspective becomes discernment… but not yet. That is and will be, hopefully, a conclusion in "the future now".

As mentioned above, artistic practitioners are particularly prone and vulnerable to starting fights when perhaps more measured words (or even silent restraint) should prevail. On Friday 20 October 1967, the actor Richard Burton records in his diary events of a few days before. On the previous Sunday he had been reading poetry at the Oxford Union, receiving a standing ovation for his performance of "Boast of Dai Greatcoat", an extract from the seven-part narrative poem about the First World War, *In Parenthesis* by David Jones; the poem was based on Jones's combat experiences as an infantryman in the Royal Welch Fusiliers on the Western Front.

Reading alongside Burton was W. H. Auden. To the sonorous, theatrically endowed Welshman, famed for his recording of Dylan Thomas's *Under Milk Wood*, Auden's attempts at verse speaking were "colourless". The actor adds, without qualifying evidence, "He is not a nice man." As a harbinger of the first punch thrown in a pub fight, more verbal assaults against poets followed in the diary disclosure. T. S. Eliot, Louis MacNeice, and both the Thomas boyos, R. S. and Dylan, receive gradations of character duffing-up. Drunkenness, animosity and jealousy were the general accusations. In Eliot's case, Burton hammers the American's renditions of his own poems, delivered "with such monotony as to stun the brain". To my knowledge, Eliot's views on Richard Burton remain unrecorded.

While it would be my first-hand observation that some poets I've encountered are not immune to the transgressions of excessive soaking of the liver, malice, and envy of their fellow poets' successes – poetry after all is a competitive business and places at the table are limited – I have also found, in the company of a fair few poets, a fellowship and finesse of respect toward one another that heartens, especially among those who have learned over the years to effectively perform their poems.

In my experience, positive encounters with accomplished poets lead to, to use Carol's phrase, "currents of connection", reaping rich insights and mutual thankfulness for the communion. One such enjoyably charged contact was with the Scottish-born poet Alastair Reid, who died in 2014 at the age of eighty-eight. We got to know Alastair during the last decade of his life through my association with the Wigtown Book Festival, for which I served as a director for a brief period, circa 2009/2010, while based in Scotland.

Prior to those duties, from the early 2000s onward I performed at that festival, and subsequently enjoyed the benefits of hearing authors and poets give public readings of their latest and previous works. One stand-out event involved Alastair reading and talking about his poetry, prose and travels, and impressions accumulated during his long years away from Scotland. One poem that Alastair performed has a tangential link to my/our poem "Everything in Heaven Comes Apart", although it was written before we met Alastair.

Sometimes poems erupt with, apparently, little gestation, as a result of an experience or something said and immediately responded to. For Alastair, in the succinct brilliance of his poem "Scotland", it happened through an exchange in St Andrews with "the woman from the fish-shop" laden with the "ancient misery" of joyless, ancestral Calvinism in her pinched soul. All around them Alastair notes the jubilant summer day that saw "larks… on long thin strings of singing" while "sunlight stayed like a halo on hair".

Inviting his neighbour to participate in the brilliant gift of being alive, Alastair exclaims, "What a day it is!" The raincoated woman, parsimonious in response, utters the thrice-said curse "We'll pay for it!" The mainly Scottish audience in the packed hall at the book festival groaned with recognition – a truth about themselves had been spoken. On behalf of his tribe, the poet had exposed, and expertly ridiculed, a tartan dybbuk. As novelist and fellow Scot Andrew O'Hagan discerned in his introduction to *Outside In* (a selection of Alastair's prose), Reid is "a modernist with an ancient heart".

Alastair's "Scotland", like the most incisive jokes, delivers microscopic exactitude of character and situation. But the poem is also a grief, a despatch of intense disappointment and even bereavement: life's munificence deflated by Calvinistic, flesh-despising dualism. As Alastair revealed in our many wide-ranging conversations over the years, he left his country in order to get away, in part, from the stultifying aridness of religion, those "evenings doomed by bells". And yet, paradoxically, as a son of the manse, he wrote of his 1930s Galloway upbringing with Eden-like idyllic rapture, in which his beloved father (as well as GP mother) faithfully served the God-fearing but not necessarily God-liking rural congregants.

Alastair's learning was terrific and instructive, conveyed in edited sentences of flair, much humour, and erudition. His studies at university were interrupted by war service in the Royal Navy, returning to St Andrews later to complete his degree. And then, as they say in the fine debating hostelries of Glasgow, it was "offski" – to the New World and a remarkable rambling life.

The files of *The New Yorker* state that Alastair wrote over 100 pieces for America's revered literary magazine during a sixty-year period. This journal became Alastair's point of call, his common room: a base camp to which he returned after one of his expeditions to Latin, and Central, America, or following a protracted stay in London, or Mallorca, where he came into the orbit of poet and classicist Robert Graves. This led to Alastair becoming Graves' on-the-road factotum on an American lecture tour when, in 1956, the author of *I, Claudius* gathered in the dollars to help pay for his children's pressing school fees.

Back on shore leave at *The New Yorker*, Alastair swapped travel stories and book business gossip with fellow contributors W. H. Auden, John Updike, and J. D. Salinger – all under the benign, studious, and probably perfect editorship of William Shawn, who let his writers get on with whatever they wanted to write about, trusting them to do so with panache and scholarly enlightenment.

One incredible story Alastair told me (and later reported by Alan Taylor in the Glasgow daily *The Herald*) had us both rolling in our respective aisles when we considered its sitcom possibilities. It concerned J. D. Salinger.

In 1951, in the run-up to the publication of the novel that voiced American post-war teenage alienation, *The Catcher in the Rye* (which Alastair had read in manuscript form before its publication), the book's jumpy author – wishing to escape the impending publicity hoo-hah – was canvassing colleagues for some escape tips. Alastair's helpful suggestion was to head east to the west coast of Scotland. What better than the bracing summer breezes of the Isle of Bute and a stay in a homely B&B? Use of cruet, sixpence extra.

Being drawn to the possibilities offered by the comically incongruous, I suggested to Alastair a scene where the landlady in a Maggie Smith/*The Prime of Miss Jean Brodie* accent enquired of literature's soon-to-become most accomplished recluse, "Tell me, Mr Say-linge-er, will you be requiring a tattie scone at breakfast tomorrow? I was disappointed to note that you hardly touched the nutritious benefit this morning. What with us still in the fearsome grip of rationing… and what have you." Alastair's twinkling eyes and generous laughter in response to this absurdity remains a merry memory for me.

Salinger did not linger long in Scotland. He returned to America, and the rest is virtually silence. Holden Caulfield's scribe retreated to Cornish in New Hampshire, where the rapidly diminishing guest list of visitors became exasperated by Salinger's increasingly stringent control. One deal was that if, at the given time, any invitee standing on the street had anyone with them – it could have coincided with a stranger stopping to ask the time – Salinger would drive past without stopping, the agreement perceived by him to have been violated.

The psychological gouges that fame inflicts dictated that Salinger about-turned from media mobbing, hunkering down in his New England hermitage. In the intervening years, the Salinger-enigma has seen a posse of medical professionals and academics theorizing and guessing. Some have detected post-traumatic stress disorder in Salinger's behavioural patterns and writings, arising from his D-Day combat with the 4th Counter Intelligence Corps detachment on Utah Beach. Salinger's war duties also included being witness to the Nazi concentration camps – enough for any sensitive individual. (My father witnessed similar, in his case Bergen-Belsen as a commando, and I consider this a major contributory factor in his far-too-early death from an "exploded heart" at the age of fifty-one.) The writer Joyce Carol Oates defined *The Catcher in the Rye* as about "the moral rootlessness of contemporary American materialism". Alastair's summing up of his colleague was, "He had come to distrust virtually everyone."

Alastair Reid has also attracted the cultural commentator's gaze. As well as being a superb poet and finely tuned expert travel writer, some discerned an almost supersensory homesickness in him, irrespective of where he was. His travels led to his becoming an outstanding Spanish linguist and the favoured translator of Chilean poet and winner of the 1971 Nobel Prize for Literature, Pablo Neruda, whom Alastair first met at Isla Negra in Chile in 1964. Alastair also provided similar, lucid service for Argentinian poet Jorge Luis Borges.

As it was Carol who initiated contact with Alastair in Wigtown's Main Street during that very special festival in 2004, Alastair duly memorialized the aligning of our planets. In his inscription to *On the Blue Shore of Silence: Poems of the Sea*, Alastair wrote in the fore-leaf, "Carol's book etc etc etc… devotedly, Alastair." And as a deterrent to any prospective light-fingered browser, his admonishment in block capitals is DO NOT REMOVE.

In his latter years, a small apartment in Greenwich Village became Alastair's home with his partner, the award-winning film-maker Leslie Clark. Their summers consisted of vacations on a farm in Garlieston, Galloway, with visits to old pals in Edinburgh and London part of the itinerary.

From his first poetry collection in 1953, *To Lighten My House*, through to *Weathering* in the late 1970s, Alastair held true to the poet's course of writing in order "to set the poems free". His yearly schlepps back to South West Scotland, and to the Isle of Whithorn in particular – where his parents once ministered and where he, as a boy, romped in "the oat and barley fields that lay between our house and the sea" – rekindled the muse. The greater "homesickness" that I believe we all carry but cannot always articulate was in Alastair's case receiving soothing comfort. In a 2010 letter to us, Alastair enthused about writing new poems, "the first for ages… Just being in Galloway brings it on". Alastair's approach to poetry was that it *had* to be written but that it would let you know *when*.

"Everything…" has had a long life since its "liberation" back in the early 1990s: first as a performance piece, with a wonderfully atmospheric musical backing entitled "Novus Magnificat" by the American ambient composer Constance Demby, which Carol and I have aired at various gigs and festivals over the years and has remained in our repertoire. It was then published in my 1997 collection, *Limited Edition*. Songwriter Martyn Joseph then took a shine to the words, contributing a distinctive melody and vocal interpretation, including it in many of his performances, and on several albums.

Remarking on the quiddity of childhood, Alastair Reid once wrote that children reside in a "limitless present" while adulthood brings "a shifting, elusive question mark". Without me knowing at the time, I think "Everything…" is an amalgam of both those states… and a hint at a more restful more. Nothing like poetry to pin things down, and then let them go.

EVERYTHING IN HEAVEN COMES APART

Everything in Heaven comes apart.
The atom and the tsetse fly,
deceits which we now justify.
The zebra's stripe, the callous joke,
the anthem that the bullfrogs croak.
The nightingale, the damning phrase,
the unseen rage of all our days.
The beetle's brain, the sour jibe,
the self-advancement moral bribe.
The leper's soul, the withered heart.
Everything in Heaven comes apart.

Comes apart, explains itself and shows its complex ways.
To see at last is to be free from our complicated maze.
And everything that's chained will come apart.

Everything in Heaven comes apart.
The tuning fork, the afternoon,
the anxious scowl of each baboon.
The bottle brush, the swing-top bin,
the lumps that grow beneath our skin.
The roulette wheel, conspiring talk,
the rhythm of the penguin's walk.
The years of grief, the libellous hint,
the plasma of the innocent.
The untraced lie, the verbal dart.
Everything in Heaven comes apart.

Comes apart, explains itself and shows its complex ways.
To see at last is to be free from our complicated maze.
And everything that's chained will come apart.

Everything in Heaven comes apart.
The pogo stick, the monkey gland,
the bloody strife fought over land.
The private scam, the public face,
the press-release attempt at grace.
The olive branch, the passport queue,
the fifteen-minute super-loo.
The parrot's blink, the gamma ray,
the things the dead would like to say…
The daffodil, the words that smart.
Everything in Heaven comes apart.

Comes apart, explains itself and shows its complex ways.
To see at last is to be free from our complicated maze.
And everything that's chained will come apart.

Everything in Heaven comes apart.
The diamond ring, the ocean's song,
the conversation that went wrong.
The dry-stone wall, the forest fire,
the smile that turned into desire.
The rising sun, the chain-store suit,
the blank gaze of the destitute.
The tender kiss, the pious mask,
the questions that we meant to ask.
The plans we had but couldn't start.
Everything in Heaven comes apart.

Comes apart, explains itself and shows its complex ways.
To see at last is to be free from our complicated maze.

And everything that's chained will come apart…
And everything that's locked will come apart…
And everything that's bound will come apart…
For everything, in Heaven, comes apart.

18

THUNDER AND RAINBOWS

A few years ago I was leading a day of poetry workshops in a primary school in eastern England. My first appointment of the morning was with the reception class. For those not familiar with primary-school speak, that means a cross-legged, wondrous tribe of inquisitive four-year-olds. Reception clans are not my natural constituency, mainly because they're generally as bright as sequins and exercise a shuddering ability to ask the kind of conceptual question that would cause Einstein to scribble down some hurried equations – such as, "How does a sleeping monkey know when it's time to wake up?"

Break off into discussion groups and consider that stumper. One acceptable answer would be (and it was the best I could come up with): if and when the dozing primate falls off its branch and crashes to the ground. So that means it's not asleep any more. Ergo – the time to wake up has suddenly arrived and let us now hurriedly move on before my young inquisitors realize they're being entertained by a right old bonehead. And you thought the life of a four-year-old was dominated by routines of biscuits, juice, and playtime. Not so – every one an infant think tank.

So, going on the basis that every mountaineer has to start somewhere, I tentatively began my expedition with this particular pack of genies with the question, "What are poems?" Now, adults perhaps hearing the voices of disapproving teachers in the classrooms of memory would hesitate in answering this question, sensing that there is the "right" answer or the self-esteem-sapping "wrong" answer. However, there were no such inhibitions with this beaming gang because they still instinctively knew that childhood is not about restriction but expanse. Hands shot up and I began to canvas their immediate, enthusiastic findings. Three answers in, and a small mystic suggests that poems "are messages". Ponder this. She is four years old and she has sent me a message about poems being messages.

I have read chin-stroking books about the meaning of poetry and the mechanics of verse, not least James Fenton's excellent *An Introduction to English Poetry*. I've gone out of my way to listen to lectures where I've taken extensive notes about enjambments, dactyls, and elisions. I've pursued my poetic apprenticeship with determination – crafting acrostics, sonnets, and deliberately (and not so deliberately) duff doggerel as part of the training. But a tiny untutored girl in Lincolnshire gave me a nigh on complete definition of a poem: the distillation of its essentiality. Poems are directives, tidings, news about ourselves, and issues concerning our place in the rapid, passing scheme of things. Poems are the manifestos of the heart and soul, opinion-editorials chiselled down into spare metre and meaning. Poems are indeed messages written by practitioners at the various stages of their literary and emotional development, sometimes one superseding or coalescing with the other.

Just as there are musicians who play by ear and feel, and others who earnestly learn the scales, so there are poets who do likewise, simultaneously. I suppose I've evolved into a from-the-heart merchant who has also tried to apply the necessary homework. Poet, journalist, and former Oxford Professor of Poetry James Fenton makes the point that in the craft of writing poetry, the poet can never arrive at completion. Poets cannot produce a certificate that states an 80 per cent pass mark has been reached. The "proof" of a poem's success is, I would suggest: does it resonate with a hearer or reader, and, irrespective of the period of history in which a poem was written, does the poem continue to echo with authenticity?

For example, four lines from the nineteenth-century poet Christina Rossetti carry a present-day pitch of clarity, acting as a contemporary comment on how outward symbols of our day, the baubles of attainment, become of no account when compared to the hidden, purifying qualities of the apparently unremarkable. "A diamond is a brilliant stone, to catch the world's desire; An opal holds a fiery spark; but a flint holds fire." The writer of "In the Bleak Midwinter" reminds us that a jagged stone, a sliver of scree, is not what it seems. Rossetti is sending us a message, a subtle memo, that what has market value may not have lasting worth, and nor should we be bluffed by its enticing riches. A, latterly, Victorian woman who was born in the reign of William IV is passing on her pithy critique, a salient social comment comparable to her modern-day "bangin'" spoken-word sisters such as Kate Tempest and Hollie McNish.

Christina Rossetti's spare and sometimes stark use of language, as in her poem "Till Tomorrow" – "Long have I longed, till I am tired Of longing and desire; Farewell my points in vain desired, My dying fire: Farewell all things that die and fail and tire" – has been a returning, abundant territory for me, especially when I've been faffing about at the borders of metaphysics. A member of a high-achieving artistic family, she was a published poet by the age of seventeen. The wider, prevailing patriarchal empire may have expected her due submission and seemly, temperate behaviour, but the precocious Rossetti was an independent thinker – an "issue" poet decades before the phrase became feature-portrait shorthand. The range of concerns in her poetry is striking, as too are the social issues she supported, such as the age of sexual consent, antivivisection, and female emancipation. Her natural introspection wedded to a personal brooding for a divine and loving moderator, an advocate of restorative justice, made Christina Rossetti a moral modernist and courageous campaigner in and outside her time.

Christina Rossetti was a "heart technician" whose economy of language attests to a life of staring at the small things of existence in order to prise meaning out of the insignificant, be it a dead mouse or a luscious hedgerow strawberry feasted on by a snail. In the emotional ascension of Rossetti's poem "A Birthday", further nature study and expressive identification with an orchard's gratuities, she likens her heart to "an apple-tree, Whose boughs are bent with thickset fruit".

Such microscopic inspections as practised by Christina Rossetti and researching of the depths result in poems breaching the surface. How the poem is then formed following this scrutiny is up to the individual poet. My poem at the end of this chapter, "Thunder and Rainbows", is message-like and seemed to come from nowhere: pondered over and planed down in the workshop of the imagination but written, I remember, in one draft, which is not always the case. It was first published in my collection *Still, facing Autumn*, published in 2000. It was then musically adopted by Martyn Joseph, who made it the title of his album *Thunder and Rainbows – The Best We Could Find*, also released in 2000. The poem/song has subsequently appeared on several of Martyn's later albums.

As a poem, it is verbal minimalism, using contrasts to address the message of how opposites can resemble the front and back flaps of a book, the pages in between measuring the progress both away and toward such states as the "bitter or sweet". All this conflict and uncertainty is taking place beneath a sky that manifests a similar antithesis, so the poem's polarities mirror nature's template, with the rainbow representing the ebbing of the thunder's fearsome percussion, the promise of calm and settlement. I think if I were writing the poem now I would attempt to incorporate the further, rare wonder of lightning and rainbows coexisting in the same sky, as caught by American photographer Greg McCown and verified by the meteorology department of Arizona State University.

At the time of writing the poem, I followed the Sylvia Plath recollection of writing like a child again in a state of "what being little feels like". Also, I remember from my mind's-eye "big book of rainbows" ones seen over the years – one colossal production in particular I watched off Orkney when I was up there making a radio feature about one of the islands' Neolithic burial sites at Maeshowe. On that thunderous day, the bright bugle of the sky was an ancient mythic blast and raising of the dead.

A further meaning behind the thunder and rainbows metaphor is that we are and become our own contrasting weather forecasts, our own extremes. Not being given to explaining poems too much in the fear that they may disappear, the child in me doesn't want to know how a spectacular magic trick is done in case "the magic disappears". And although the rational adult in me is equally intrigued by the misdirection required to execute an illusion, what "Thunder and Rainbows" does is locate and note the swings of temperament that multiple and variable circumstances can cause in us.

Depending on the "weather conditions", we can become either the enemy or the friend or someone inhabiting the no-fixed point in the many stages between – the positive, the neutral, or the negative. That's not to say we remain permanently at the unfavourable end of the spectrum; "Thunder and Rainbows" just recognizes that sometimes we do end up there. The words are, I would like to think, like a life coach who counsels, "Don't stay there, because you are not being the best of yourself – your 'intended being'. Find your way away from there."

Fans of the film *The Wizard of Oz* will pick up on the obvious reference to the yellow brick road in what became the chorus for the song. Keen theologians (is there any other type? A disgruntled one? Half-hearted? All over the place?) will recognize the Christian symbolism of "the throne and the tree": the disparate images of Christ's demise and dawning encapsulated in five words, which is something of a reductionist disservice and an inadequate representation of what is, for Christians, the salvation narrative. I plead Tom Stoppard's Guildenstern character in defence: "words [are] all we have to go on" – at length or in brevity. Having set a spartan technical structure, I had to stick to it, m'lud.

From the earliest cuneiform characters transcribed by the Sumerians some 3,000–5,000 years ago to the digital equivalent of today – the text – humankind has written and continues to write messages; the meaning or lack of it is in the script, the shape, and the substance of the words. Kindly read the following message; it's yours to deliberate over, or discard, in keeping with its divergent concepts.

THUNDER AND RAINBOWS

The light and the shade
concealed or displayed
enemies, friends
opposite ends.
Bitter or sweet
ruffled or neat
feathers or lead
silent or said.

Generous or mean
corporate or green
vagrant or lord
the dove or the sword.
Distinct or obscure
prosperous or poor
devil or saint
we are and we ain't.

Intricate mysteries
life's secret codes
Cul-de-sac signposts
on yellow brick roads
Ambiguous answers –
the question's still: "Why?"
Thunder and rainbows
from the same sky

Champagne or dust
banquet or crust
authentic or fake
angel or snake.
Flower or thorn
pristine or torn
desert or sea
the throne and the tree.

Intricate mysteries
life's secret codes
Cul-de-sac signposts
on yellow brick roads
Ambiguous answers –
the question's still: "Why?"
Thunder and rainbows
from the same sky

19

CONSIDERATION /
I WISH YOU...

The Italian film director Federico Fellini, who died in 1993, regarded art as, primarily, autobiography. He asserted this theory by regarding the pearl as being "the oyster's autobiography". There is an oil-on-canvas painting by the Russian Jewish artist Marc Chagall entitled *Promenade*, created toward the end of the First World War, that is one such enraptured autobiographical statement.

I've chosen the painting as a rhapsodic portal into this special, personal chapter, which has not one but two poems at its culmination. The poems are attempts, in a shorthand of the heart, to convey how much "I would not have been as much, or anywhere at all" if not for the sustaining love, support, and selfless devotion and commitment of my wife, Carol. This chapter is a testimony to how much she breathes and bounds through many of the poems I've produced down the decades, and through over forty years of marriage. We have very personal, geographically related memories associated with Marc Chagall too, which I'll tell of later.

By the time that his love-letter painting *Promenade* had been completed, Chagall, lowly born, had been married to Bella Rosenfeld, from a prosperous Orthodox Jewish family, for a couple of years. They had been blessed with the birth of a daughter, Ida, in 1916, the year following their match. In later life, Ida went on to curate exhibitions of her father's works, and in

1990, four years before her death, she bequeathed over 100 works by Chagall to the Israel Museum in Jerusalem.

Promenade portrays Chagall and Bella in intriguing, allegorical communion. He is looking "straight to camera", finely suited with legs sturdily apart, his face emitting an expansive smile of hope and happiness. He is holding the hand of Bella, who, in a full-length light-purple dress, is floating above her husband – a low hovering human kite, a symbol of ethereal contentment. The painting's sentiment is an affirmation of how hallowed human relationship can become elevated symbiosis. Above them the smeared light of sky is an aerial prospect of almost mellow-brooding with its faint hues of darkness – a storm coming?

In the foreground of the painting at Chagall's right foot is a lavishly coloured picnic blanket in patterned red, with a wine decanter and single goblet. Meanwhile, behind the two lovers in shades of rich and subtle green are the pastures and buildings of their home settlement, Vitebsk (now in present-day Belarus). In Chagall and Bella's day, Vitebsk, his mythic palette, was part of the Imperial Russian empire within the Pale of Settlement, with a population of somewhere between 60,000 and 70,000, about half of whom were Jewish.

But the years surrounding the creation of *Promenade* were far from ones of settled contentment. Violence and domestic foment rattled the days. Under the prohibitive rule of Tsar Nicholas II, Russia was in perilous decline, a poverty pandemic. When full revolution did finally erupt in October 1917 following the Tsar's abdication, the murderous snuffing out of the royalist regime bred the profound uncertainty of change. In the new order, not even the primary revolutionaries were safe from the paranoid suspicions of their comrades. The confounding virus of anti-Semitism continued, embedding itself in the fledgling system. For history wearily tutors us that such specific ethnic detestation and scapegoating infects all points on the ideological spectrum, from regal dictatorship to totalitarian liberalism.

As members of the Jewish community, Marc and Bella's immediate forebears had endured regular pogroms, as well as the inevitable restrictions of movement. These shackles, however, were eased a little during the Great War years, enabling the newly-weds to move to and reside in Petrograd (later Saint Petersburg) in the autumn of 1915. By day, Chagall's alternative military service consisted of working in the War Economy Bureau. In his truncated free time in Russia's second city he built on his burgeoning artistic reputation that had begun through showings of his work in Paris in 1915, and the year before in Berlin. Prior to Ida's birth, Chagall exhibited in a gallery in Petrograd, run by his friend and pioneer art dealer Nadezhda Dobychina.

The French writer and one of the original members of the Dadaist group of surrealists André Breton described Chagall as *the* father of surrealism. Through Chagall, Breton affirmed, "Metaphor made its triumphal entry into modern painting." For a short period after the Russian Revolution, Chagall, as a vanguard of the avant-garde, enjoyed a brief season of acceptance by the proletarian establishment.

But by the beginning of 1924, with Lenin dead, to be replaced by the "worker's tsar" – Stalin – art was soon to be insidiously subjected to approval and censure by committee. The propaganda of socialist realism became the representative gallery. What place for a parabolic visionary like Chagall who painted from deep within, ignoring the expected promulgation of the State? The Chagall family, intuitively sensing the restrictions and possible houndings to come, went into exile in 1922, first to Berlin, then Paris, and like "the wandering Jew", a recurring motif in his post-Russia paintings, to wherever his art would take them.

While only in her early fifties, Bella died of a viral infection in 1944 in New York. In the bleak months of mourning that followed, Chagall's heart became a blank canvas, and he was unable to create. In his later years, Chagall, commemorating his earthly muse depicted in *Promenade*, said of Bella, "She has flown over my pictures for many years, guiding my art." Substitute the word poems for pictures, and I say the same about Carol.

And here I take up the geographical inventory referred to earlier, of places we've both stood, and sat, in silence, letting Chagall's dreamlike compositions minister their grandeur and subtle glory. The first occasion was at Smith College in Northampton, Massachusetts, in the early 1990s, when, on the day after a poetry gig in the town, with a delighted shock we were casually shown by our hostess a parade of Chagall drawings arranged in an unspectacular corridor on campus. We were both so stunned to see them there, I don't remember us asking how they came into the college's possession.

The next occasion was in an altogether different setting, and far more accessible – if you fancy an uplifting excursion into the Kent countryside. In All Saints' Church, Tudeley, are twelve stained-glass windows, designed by Chagall and worked on over a period of some fifteen years in collaboration with the French stained-glass master Charles Marq. The east window was the initial commission: a memorial to Sarah d'Avigdor-Goldsmid, who died, along with her boyfriend David Winn, in a sailing accident off Rye in 1963. Her parents, Sir Henry and Lady Rosemary, approached Chagall, with Lady Rosemary eventually persuading him to honour her daughter. When in 1967 Chagall visited Tudeley for the installation, he offered his services to design the other eleven windows, inspired by verses from Psalm 8. These were finally completed by 1985.

Chagall had been incorporating biblical scenes into his paintings since the early 1930s. The memorial window at Tudeley maintained this exploration with the figure of Christ on the cross, a symbol of universal and transformative suffering, drawing the viewer's eye upward at the apex. At the base of the scene, the lucid blue swell of the sea holds a woman's body at rest. The window is a visceral example of art fulfilling one of its important ideals – empathy in grief, assimilation of loss.

Chagall had previously captured this representation of consuming suffering with Christ as a central effigy in his harrowing painting *White Crucifixion*, presently on display at The Art Institute of Chicago. Here Chagall interprets Jesus as unmistakeably Jewish, the traditional loincloth replaced by a prayer shawl, his historically reported crown of thorns substituted with a head cloth. To the martyr's left, a Torah and synagogue are engulfed in the flames of persecution. If one of art's intentions is to enable "a different seeing", Chagall succeeds. It is a painting, like a sagacious poem, to return to and receive the wisdom of further meaning. Toward the end of his life, Chagall reflected, "… that is how I understood him… under the influence of the pogroms. Then I painted and drew him in pictures about ghettoes, surrounded by Jewish troubles…"

Our most recent concord with the full, brilliant flair of Chagall took place on our latest visit to Jerusalem in 2014. Starting at the familiar Damascus Gate, a pitta pocket bulging with falafel for every time we've entered and exited the Old City by that route down the years, we travelled up to the Hadassah University Medical Center in Ein Kerem, West Jerusalem. In all the years, going back to my first trip in 1974 (Carol had been on earlier occasions), that we visited, and stayed, in the city, this was the first time we had entered the Abbell Synagogue. Chagall's dozen stained-glass windows – again working in partnership with Charles Marq – dedicated to the historical tribes of Israel, starting with Reuben and through to Benjamin, are astounding, each window absorbing the sun's light and intensifying its chosen churning colour. Art as blessing, a series of thematic beatitudes of Jacob on his twelve sons, and Moses on the tribes of Israel.

This chapter is, indeed, about blessing – mine, in sharing a life of abundance with Carol. And while our meaningful, mystical association with Chagall is just a few pages from our long life together, I would like to leave you with one of my many sacred memories of her.

After a period of too many years of Carol being besieged by major illnesses, and including enduring severe injuries resulting from a car crash and subsequent prolonged incapacitation, a cherished time in New York in 1994 exemplifies for me her tenacity, courage, and resolve in restoring these locust times.

We had been invited by the author and winner of the prestigious Newbery Medal for children's literature in 1963, Madeleine L'Engle, to stay and celebrate Thanksgiving in her Manhattan apartment. This was a great honour as it was exclusively "en famille". During our treasured time with Madeleine we learned something of her early writing struggles, not least how the several million-seller *A Wrinkle in Time* had been rejected by over twenty publishers before being taken in off the streets by Farrer, Straus and Giroux in 1962.

To be in Madeleine's reserved presence was, if she took to you, to walk under the canopy of acceptance, judicious insight, and vast kindness. Knowing something of Carol's "war service", Madeleine asked if there was anything Carol would like to do over the holiday period during the day. Carol said she'd like to ride a horse through Central Park. A phone call from Madeleine and off we traipsed to a high-rise overlooking the park. Looking up we found it difficult to imagine horses being stabled inside, and I visualized the beautifully bizarre sight of a horse poking his head out of his several-storeys-high stall, viewing the neighbourhood with his city-wise equine eyes, then blowing raspberries at those newfangled skateboarders slaloming through the park.

The allocated horse (a dappled grey named "Birch") was, however, brought to street level from a subterranean "paddock" of the building (rising regally, ears coming into view first, in a mammoth lift), saddled and girthed and ready for a constitutional. On hearing Carol's English accent, the stable owner had her down as a skilled horsewoman, which she is, and said, to Carol's intense delight, "Off you go on your own." Being holiday time, the traffic in central Manhattan was steady. Carol did the equivalent of flicking the horse's indicator and off she went into the fall-fathoms of Central Park. This, a woman who, following the referred-to-earlier car smash, had broken a bone in her neck and was told that in all probability she might never walk again. She had the exuberant look of a child who'd been told sunflowers can sing – and would she like to join in with them?

An hour or so later, rider and horse emerged, at one, at peace, and I glowed with immeasurable pride. So, if the first poem strikes you as a tad on the sad side, please don't read it as such. It's a poem of gratitude, of treasuring blessing, and the anticipation of a "flawless shore" for her, and me, some day sooner... or later.

CONSIDERATION

No one ever told me that grief felt so like fear.
C. S. Lewis

I could bear anything
but the ending of you.
Yet should that come to pass –
the indentation in the sofa
your comb and signet ring
the magnifying mirror full of portraits of you
the functioning house, the haven of days –
these would be my well-being
my saints' bones
the decree that you are and are
the statute of the boundless.

Don't know what I'd do though,
but love you even more.
I would sweep the path in autumn
and feed the roses;
those would be my rituals
my lighting of candles.
And I would be hollow and whole
because of you.

I WISH YOU...

I wish you Temple true
and all of deep content.
I wish you royal rare,
a lasting covenant.

I wish you citadels
and keeps of love and space.
I wish you everlasting
in this temporary place.

I wish you solitude,
a Yosemite of grace.
I wish you plenteous,
an immutable embrace.

I wish you realms and spheres,
and dawn that will be yours.
I wish you luminous…
then Heaven's flawless shores.

20

THE CATS OF JERUSALEM

This chapter entails various links in a chain – strategic phone calls made but, obviously, without the detailed foreknowledge of how things may develop as a result, highlighting the curious and correlative outcomes that strategy and chance can bring about. The culminating poem this time probably began over forty years ago through watching feral cats slink and scurry through the walled city of Jerusalem. The creatures in the poem are metaphors for conflict and the next generation of unreason, embodying the perpetuation of septic, violent argument over land.

But before the consideration of that verse – once upon a time... Back in the early 1990s, I was on the promotional-interview trail following the release of my second book of poetry for Hodder & Stoughton, *Homeland*. My adept publicist for that campaign, Geraldine Perry, secured an appearance for me on a BBC Radio Scotland magazine menagerie programme entitled *Eddie Mair Live*. The evening before, I had given a poetry performance at the Scottish Exhibition Centre in Glasgow and had spoken to the radio programme's producer, Stewart Easton, to finalize the following morning's arrangements.

At an early-bird hour when semi-conscious larks were blearily consulting their songbook, I turned up at the studios – a labyrinth multitasking as a warren on Queen Margaret Drive. I had mentioned to Stewart E. the idea of writing a poem based on the items featured in the programme that morning. This went down well, making a change from the generally accepted book plug etiquette, "this is my masterpiece, don't leave home without it". The "instant" poem attraction suggested was not an original idea; the exceptional lyric poet Nigel Forde had perfected the form on BBC Radio 4's *Midweek* for several years. I canvassed tips from Nigel as to how best carry on the tradition north of the border. Nigel was generous with his advice and inside gen on how to go about the task: ascertain the programme's running order beforehand.

There was an eclectic guest list to draw on that day, including an interview with Conservative MP for Billericay from 1987 to 2001, the forthright and always entertaining Teresa Gorman, who finally handed in her mortal Order Paper in 2015. (Teresa Gorman was an – ahem – "conviction politician" who could be called upon to enliven the snooziest of afternoons in the Commons; a Thatcherite foot soldier, self-made businesswoman, devout Eurosceptic, and an effervescent apostle for hormone replacement therapy. This latter benefit introduced bemused club-land shire Tories to the wholly unfamiliar parliamentary subject of the menopause. Mrs Gorman later became a backbench bother to Margaret Thatcher's successor, John Major, who expelled her (for five months) from the Party in 1994, along with eight other "insubordinates", for refusing to fall into line over Major's pragmatic line on Europe.)

The Scottish international goalkeeper Andy Goram was also in the line-up, along with music from that most excellent of Scottish singer-songwriters, Carol Laula.

Thankfully I didn't make a poodle's petit déjeuner of the whole enterprise, and Eddie and his production playmates encouraged me to the point of inviting me back the following week for more of the same. This continued for a few more outings until producer Caroline Barbour floated the idea of a weekly four-minute diary piece entitled *The Days of Pearl E. Spencer*. Some of you synth-pop partisans will remember Marc Almond's 1992 hit "The Days of Pearly Spencer", from which Caroline derived her blistering idea. (Because of my impressive vintage I vividly remember the 1967 original, written by Belfast-born troubadour David McWilliams. The hit of that summer, played on a loop by Radio Caroline.)

I asked Caroline (the producer, not the pirate radio station), "Who is Pearl?" Back came an answer along the lines of – she's a chiffon-scarfed English actress at a difficult age. I embellished further. For example, Pearl had neglected to update her portrait photograph in *Spotlight,* the actor's casting catalogue. Her starlet days had been spent in 1950s repertory theatre, adorned by character parts in British B-movies. The acting profession being a sparse banquet, Pearl, not long divorced, was now marooned on modest means in the whizz-bang fashion fireworks of early-1990s Glasgow, European Capital of Culture.

Thanks to Caroline, I was dealt an ace hand. I became Pearl's secretary, informing her fans each week of her transformation from previous breathless entrances through the French windows, via the tennis court, in Rattigan-like dramas to rehearsing in a squalid Portakabin in Parkhead in an edgy urban-gothic production with, according to Pearl, "Some rather revolting dialogue to deliver… without wincing." And, oh! how Celia Johnson – not one of Pearl's profit-share fellow actors bothered with vocal warm-ups – would shudder. Scandalously unprofessional.

Young therapist Magenta became a vague, sweet recurring confessional as Pearl attempted to make sense of her life. Yet Dame Fortune came knocking on Fate's dressing room door, with Pearl landing a telly part in the lunchtime serial *Blether in the Heather*. Any similarity to STV's high-ratings rural soap opera of the time, *Take the High Road*, was affectionately deliberate. In the melodramatic spirit of these things, after several months of Pearl's adventures, I killed her off when one fateful day in *Blether…* a runaway tractor "squashed her from the bosom downward".

Actors' jokes and references were crowbarred into the script with some new jests besides. Pearl enjoyed a run of several months on the wireless, broadcast live, just like the first series of *Doctor Who* (in which Pearl had appeared as a Voord warrior (series 5) in black-and-white 1964… "Dear Bill Hartnell, such a chum," Pearl would recall).

However, the true, lasting fortune from those festive days was meeting E. Mair, Esq., Dundee's very own gentleman broadcaster and seamless presenter. Although Eddie, showing his trademark impeccable timing, left the programme shortly after my arrival, taking his name with him, our precious friendship was forged during those remarkable radio days. It has continued personally and professionally for over twenty-five years. With a fan's shared enthusiasm for country music and Mel Brooks – Jewish barroom ballads, anyone? – we make each other laugh, sometimes helplessly, yet most importantly: Eddie has been a sensitive counsel, when I whinge on about something professionally minor; a generous and discreet listener who was a key, big-hearted culprit in getting me into further radio scrapes, for which I am, as they rarely say in all the best obituaries, eternally grateful.

Eddie and I have since made feature documentaries for Radio 4 together in conjunction with Jo Coombs (who will feature further in a few paragraphs' time) as executive producer and fellow (fellowette?) Bash Street Kid. I regard those programmes, such as documentaries on the life of Lionel Bart, the Celtic roots of country music, and the history of the SOS message service on BBC Radio, as among my happiest and most worthwhile times in radio.

When Eddie was on the cusp of taking the road south to BBC 5 Live following *EML* winning a Gold Sony Radio Academy Award (the big school of Radio 4 came later with an illuminated cabinet of more completely unnecessary awards), he was presenting *Breakaway*, the then Saturday morning travel programme on Radio 4 made by the same department as the Friday evening feature travelogue *Going Places* (produced by David Prest, who doubled up on both programmes, I seem to remember). Are you following this? I am. David says to Eddie (I paraphrase), "Do you know anyone who can hold a microphone the right way up and possesses a winning hint of quirk?" Eddie very kindly recommended yours truly. That's how it was done back then. No training course required, just an assumed ethos of public service broadcasting and the instruction to, when required, try to make the prosaic sizzle.

On my first assignment for *Going Places*, I was sent off to the Palace of Westminster to interview MPs with fascinating hobbies. One backbencher regarded supporting York City as thrilling as striding into the Mother of Parliaments. Gyles Brandreth, then the Member for Chester, skipped around the nursery with his extensive knowledge of Steiff teddy bears. Another who stepped onto the captain's bridge was SNP *Star Trek* aficionado Roseanna Cunningham. The respected Caledonian representative had to endure a howler of an opening gambit from Mr Muddle as I nervously fumbled with the microphone – a tricky, unforgiving implement. By way of warm-up, reassuring small talk, I asked the able politician if she got back to Scotland much. As priceless questions go, mine was a Fabergé egg of stupidity, seeing as her constituency was Perth and Kinross. (Production note to self – engage brain before giving the impression you haven't got one.)

More broadcasting capers followed up to 2002, when I was eventually given the presenter's role on *Questions, Questions*, taking over from the TV emperor of *Blockbusters*, Bob Holness. To quote from the Radio 4 listings spiel, *Questions, Questions* addressed "the intriguing and seemingly imponderable questions posed by everyday life". The ultimate meaning of existence evaded our enquiries, but I did get to quiz Britain's leading gooseberry expert; spend a hair-whitening afternoon outside Bristol in a clammy, claustrophobic room full of tarantulas; and discuss the philosophical principles and possible ambiguities that drive altruism with Professor A. C. Grayling in his Birkbeck College study, among other things. We made around 200 programmes. I could entertain you with other thrilling encounters… but you must have things to do.

A ten-year residency on *QQ* gave me an invaluable apprenticeship and an opportunity to make feature documentaries for not only Whistledown Productions, the company formed by David Prest when he left Radio 4 that made *QQ*, but also other companies pitching programmes to the network.

And here the fairy godmother of convergence waves her magic thingy as the poem "The Cats of Jerusalem" strolls toward us. My producer on my first few series of *QQ* was Jo Coombs (mentioned earlier). As a practitioner of her radio trade, Jo excels. For example, there is an assumption that presenters of general(ist) feature programmes fully comprehend their given brief. When you are one such befuddled luminary (that is, me), commissioned to interview a scientist with a brain the size of Mercury on the rudiments of "surface tension", one would hope for a reasonably edifying outcome – the object of the exercise being to make the mystery accessible for the listener. Not initially, in that particular case. As one whose Physics O Level answer paper resembled a chancer's exercise in guessing, what hope then of coaxing the bullet points of surface tension from a gifted interviewee?

Jo, however, exercising the saintly patience of St Brigid of Kildaire, quietly explained, and at some length, surface tension in a way that even I could grasp for about thirty seconds. I think an elastic band and a fluffy mint imperial figured in the ad hoc demonstration – or that could have been me distractedly producing items from my jacket pocket. Anyway, to quote novelist Georgette Heyer, "we brushed through" the interview "tolerably well".

So, who do you want beside you in a tension-fuelled, incense-imbued, Middle-Eastern cathedral with police and soldiers holding back excitable pilgrims from ripping an... erm... "entrepreneurial" religious patriarch to pieces? Step forward, Ms Coombs.

Following service with Whistledown, Jo gravitated to Loftus Productions, as it then was, founded by the late Nigel Acheson, an outstanding programme maker (count the awards). As his 2008 obituary in *The Guardian* so accurately described it, the fleet-of-foot Loftus set-up was "a family, a welcoming space". Those of us who made features for Nigel would all say "aye" to that.

As to how Jo and self came to be standing in the Church of the Holy Sepulchre in the Old City of Jerusalem for several hours with me jabbering away, trying to explain the complicated, heated action? Well, that would be my doing.

Some years before, I had attended the cacophonous ceremony of the Holy Fire, the celebration of the Eastern Orthodox Easter, and thought then, "This is too good for television," and made a mental note. I suggested an on-location documentary of the religious event to Nigel, who effortlessly convinced Radio 4, duly sending Jo and me off with the exquisite light-touch incentive, "Do come back with some good stuff." So that is how the pair of us came to be hemmed into the stifling press enclosure opposite the edicule: not a safe place to observe the proceedings, as it turned out. My intuition chirped up, and we ended up baling out from our allotted place, which then enabled us to wander about the vast edifice – within reason – vox-popping Bulgarian pilgrims and local Christian Palestinian families. Much better than being jammed into a precarious holding pen of film crews and fellow hacks.

It was not an easy programme to make, but it was intensely invigorating. The heightened, toxic atmosphere was exacerbated by fevered rumours in the run-up to the Holy Fire that the presiding Orthodox Patriarch, Irenaois, had been flogging off church land to Israeli investors.

Young Christian Palestinian men, outraged by the speculation, surged furiously toward the cleric as he entered the Holy Sepulchre. Israeli security forces swarmed around Irenaois, protecting him and preventing a potentially murderous brawl. The ceremony went ahead. Although the Holy Sepulchre was Level-10 tense, we focused on the project, and ended up winning a Jerusalem Radio Award.

The Israeli novelist and intellectual Amos Oz, long-committed to the two-state solution, darkly describes Jerusalem as "a black widow who devours her mates while they are still penetrating her" – that is, every empire and individual, be aware as you approach "the city of gold".

As for the poem, the last thing the rancorous wounds of Jerusalem need is yet another opinion about a wall or a security barrier or a jabbing, polarized sermon on the historical and contemporary injustices suffered by both sides. The poem is merely a "widow's mite", a pleading recognition of the plight of both tribes enmeshed in an ongoing intractable argument, for which there has to be a solution... someday... for all our sakes.

THE CATS OF JERUSALEM

The cats of Jerusalem carry, daily,
their cross of worms
a burden of fleas.
They pad through the city
from East to West and back again, languorously,
in the heat of suffering.

In the Old City
they eye chirping sprawls of sparrows
who have landed in the wrong place.
The cats of Jerusalem stretch and scratch
and attack each other,
beyond walls and checkpoints;
yowling for their feline God of the wilderness
to stroke and acquit them.
Each morning the sun rises oblivious… and yawns.

21

I HAVE GROWN AN OLD
MAN'S SKIN

I have almost written enough in this book about the validity, purpose, and importance of poetry. So, in this final chapter, I'm not so much trying to draw everything together but rather letting the conclusion be a hitching post, a stop before the ride continues over the hills and far away; ideally, to continue the equine metaphor, singing the theme tune from the 1960s television series about a talking horse, *Mister Ed.*

For those old enough to remember, let's take a moment to warble that harmony-hooved hymn, "A horse is a horse of course, of course, and no one can talk to a horse of course..." For further theological study re conversational creatures, I refer you to Numbers 22, where a short-tempered dullard called Balaam has a right old barney with his much wiser beast of burden: a put-upon ass possessing formidable powers of reason, discourse, observation, and Hebrew. Balaam confirmed his consuming rage and shaky grasp of reality, treating it as completely normal that a big-toothed mammal should be kvetching and imploring, "Stop with all the hitting." It's a cracker of a story – do look it up. But I digress...

A recent discovery on the poetic trail for Carol and me (through the writings of Richard Rohr) has been Mary Oliver, winner of the 1984 Pulitzer Prize for Poetry. At the beginning of her cathartic 2009 collection, *Evidence,* is a quote from nineteenth-century

Danish philosopher Søren Kierkegaard: "We create ourselves by our choices." Those choices have the potential to increase or lessen us. I am, of course, speaking generally here. Where the element of choice is obliterated by barrel-bombs or the brutality of oppression, then self-determination is an invisible "crown", an intangible inheritance, when suffering and diminishment is the portion. Oh, that that were not so! But I remember an effulgent woman I met in a mud-slithering Manila slum where waterborne diseases prevailed all around her shack. This diminutive saint rose each morning to sweep her miniscule floor, bathe her children in a boiled-water, spotless small bowl, and tend her vivid riot of geraniums. When I talked to her during a filming trip to the Philippines many years ago, the key to unlock her padlock of poverty was continuously lost but *her choice* was a creative, transformational act. I should continue to honour her by applying her heroic example and do likewise in my own circumstances.

We are beings of creation; creatures that choose to flourish, even in the most adverse of circumstances. And should we be so fortunate as to maintain functioning faculties into our "threescore and ten" season, then our focus can be the agent that, subsequently, gathers a new, extraordinary harvest.

Watching Carol in her luminous latter years choosing (from a standing start with no previous art history training) to study, with her inspirational diligence, and practise the centuries old art of iconography, is to watch transcendent recreation for the benefit of others. The "witness" of any shared creativity is, as I've suggested before: does the art resonate with and draw in the recipient? In Carol's case, I can affirm it has and it does in all-embracing ways, and often with dear folk who, understandably, usually dismiss religious imagery, possibly because they are "recovering Catholics or Anglicans", and so on. The church for them has "form", with some of it blighted and monstrous.

Iconography, long associated with the Eastern Orthodox Church and having evolved over centuries, is in very simple terms the pictorial representation of major characters, saints, and symbols from Christian tradition, designed especially to speak to the illiterate and wounded. The particular image presented becomes the "language from within". The icon says what the icon says. Rather like a poem, the mood and phrasing of the icon can take on different meanings for each respective viewer.

Iconography is a "figurative denomination" from which artists such as Salvador Dali have refashioned and reinterpreted the conventional tenets to cohere with their own artistic vision. For Dali in *The Sacrament of the Last Supper*, his language from within transforms the earth-rooted Upper Room into an ethereal limbo. A semi-torso above the stone table suggests the elevation of resurrection in progress. Chagall's *White Crucifixion* (commented on in Chapter 19) likewise borrows from the Russian Orthodox iconography of his native region with which he was familiar. Chagall restored, to some people's discomfort, Christ's mortal Jewishness.

Iconography's influence can be seen in the work of one of the notable American abstract expressionists, Barnett Newman, in particular, although not at first viewing. His fourteen-canvas sequence, *The Stations of the Cross*, painted over a period of eight years from the late 1950s onward, comprises stark and subtle black-and-white variations of smudged vertical lines and space with no recognizable religious symbols or characters depicted.

However, as Newman explained in the exhibition catalogue that accompanied the installation, Jesus' howling question from the cross – "*lema sabachthani*": "Why have you forsaken me?" – is, in that moment, the question that has no answer and as such connects us all to the human condition and the ultimate pertinence of existence.

The context, "moral crisis", and question that permeated Newman's paintings were framed by the numbing and draining shock of the Holocaust, and its perplexing aftermath. "After such horror, what should we paint?" In the maelstrom of our own times where the reporting of graphic carnage is instant, this is a similar conundrum for the serious and committed artist just as much as it was for Newman and his colleagues. How should we reflect the jubilee and turbulence of these days so that one does not jar with and override the other?

Iconography and its practitioners can also list repetitious persecutions and desecrations, from the days of the fledgling church onward and, specifically, following the death of Constantine in the fourth century. The craft, techniques, and procedures followed in traditional iconography are meticulously complex in process and function, handed down from "masters" (some being women) to apprentices down the centuries, and so it continues.

Carol has been fortunate to have been tutored by three exceptional exponents, Annie Shaw, Dr Irina Bradley, and Nikita Andrejev. As a non-figurative artist, it is the processes required in iconography that I find glowing with metaphors of our lives. The natural mineral and earth pigments, including semi-precious stones such as lapis lazuli, are ground down and then fused and mixed with egg yolk and white wine. The dried hard solid wood (poplar or linden tree) gesso boards – with their iceberg-white brightness formed by layer after layer of chalk and marble dust over organic linen – receive the icon image. And then the remarkable technical challenge for the artist: the gold leaf, applied very early on in the process with its metaphor of redemption as it is breathed onto an earthy base – that is, we begin pure and good and of supreme value and we become further, even though life mars and gashes in between, temporarily scarring the glister.

And so to the final poem, which began while I was shaving one morning. The hope of equilibrium is at its core, to be then, as Seamus Heaney sings, "astonished and assumed into florescence".

Enough said. These are my notes… so far.

I HAVE GROWN AN OLD MAN'S SKIN

I have grown an old man's skin
and it is good and fortunate and impermanent.
Lined now with stories, main features, and repeats;
a creased and creviced parchment
that will soon be rolled up
and tied with the knotted bow of completion.

And after that… I'm banking on…
the expansion back, the return.
A wee galaxy travelling toward the single point,
the first radiation, the Light who did not know old age
or its confirmation of such in mirrors;
whose geography while here was arduous and limited,
a reduction beyond our knowing;
the Universe diminished, the overarching Lamb,
the impaled rainbow, the pinioned magnet of grace
who in still pools or gloss marble
in the right light of His Light saw all matter reflected
back,
the nucleus and lineage of love.

I have grown an old man's skin
as agelessness cavorts within.